WISCONSIN GUIDE
for ARMED CITIZENS

HOW TO SURVIVE AN ATTACK PHYSICALLY, MORALLY, LEGALLY AND FINANCIALLY

Written by
Gene German and Tim Grant

Published by
LEOSA Trainers, Inc.

Wisconsin Guide for Armed Citizens

Published by the LEOSA Trainers, Inc.

Third Printing, June 2016

LEOSA Trainers, Inc.   TF Grant LLC
PO Box 202   4722 Forest Circle
Excelsior MN 55331   Minnetonka, MN 55345
612-388-2403   952-935-2414

10 9 8 7 6 5 4 3 2 1

Library of Congress Cataloguing-in-Publication Data

LEOSA Trainers, Inc.

ISBN 978-0-9862058-0-4

Wisconsin Guide for Armed Citizens

Printed in the United States of America by Dunn & Semington, 5250 West 73rd Street, Minneapolis, MN 55439 (612) 866-7225

Written by Gene German and Tim Grant
Design and Layout by Gene German and Tim Grant
Typesetting by Dunn & Semington

Photos by Oleg Volk and Gene German. Used by permission

Foreword

By Suzanna Hupp

I was not raised in a house with guns, and I am not a hunter. I was, however, raised in a house in which my father was an expert on the founding of this great country and I was steeped in the meaning of our Second Amendment. I grew up understanding its importance for not only protecting "We the people" from a tyrannical government, but also for the more personal reasons of protecting family, property, or even oneself. Once I began my professional life, a patient of mine who happened to be an assistant district attorney in Houston, TX convinced me to carry a gun for personal protection.

On October 16, 1991, my parents and I were eating lunch in a crowded cafeteria. As we lingered over coffee, a truck suddenly came crashing through the floor-to-ceiling window at the front of the building. The driver stepped out of the vehicle and slowly, methodically began to shooting patrons. He had complete control over the room. I remember thinking, "I've got this guy." He was standing up, everyone else was down. I have hit much smaller targets at much greater distances. I reached for the gun in my purse on the floor next to me. Then I realized that a few months earlier, I had made the stupidest mistake of my life. My gun was a hundred feet away in my car, completely useless to me. I had begun leaving it there because at that time, in the state of Texas, it was illegal to carry it and I was afraid of losing my chiropractic license.

In the end, I made it out, my parents and twenty one others did not. At that time, it was the largest mass shooting this country had ever seen.

We had not been in a dark alley on the seedy side of town. We had been in a crowded restaurant on a sunny day. I have had people say, "Suzanna, you could have missed!" and "What if your gun had jammed?" Both things were possible. But one thing no one can argue with: IT WOULD HAVE CHANGED THE ODDS.

My mother was raised in Wisconsin, brought here from a crumbling Germany by her parents. My Godmother still resides in your great state. So yes, it is personal.

I am guessing that if you are reading this book, you already believe in your right to protect yourself. However, you may have loved ones who are uncomfortable with the whole idea of guns. Have them imagine being in a restaurant when a crazed gunman enters and begins murdering innocent people. But instead of having their parents with them, let them imagine they have children or grandchildren at their sides. At the point that the gunman is leveling his weapon on their two year old's forehead, even if they have chosen not to carry a gun, don't they hope the guy behind them has one and knows how to use it?

Suzanna Gratia Hupp
Author of *From Luby's to the Legislature: One Woman's Fight Against Gun Control*

A short lesson about human nature

Col. Dave Grossman is a former West Point psychology professor, Professor of Military Science, and an Army Ranger who has combined his experiences to become the founder of a new field of scientific endeavor, which has been termed "killology." In this new field Col. Grossman has made revolutionary new contributions to our understanding of killing in war, the psychological costs of war, the root causes of the current "virus" of violent crime that is raging around the world, and the process of healing the victims of violence, in war and peace. One of Col. Grossman's more famous observations of the human condition is the perfect introduction to our book. Thank you, Col. Grossman.

On sheep, wolves and sheepdogs

One Vietnam veteran, an old retired colonel, once said this to me: "Most of the people in our society are sheep. They are kind, gentle, productive creatures who can only hurt one another by accident." This is true. Remember, the murder rate is six per 100,000 per year, and the aggravated assault rate is four per 1,000 per year. What this means is that the vast majority of Americans are not inclined to hurt one another.

Some estimates say that two million Americans are victims of violent crimes every year, a tragic, staggering number, perhaps an all-time record rate of violent crime. But there are almost 300 million Americans, which means that the odds of being a victim of violent crime is considerably less than one in a hundred on any given year. Furthermore, since many violent crimes are committed by repeat offenders, the actual number of violent citizens is considerably less than two million.

Thus there is a paradox, and we must grasp both ends of the situation: We may well be in the most violent times in history, but violence is still remarkably rare. This is because most citizens are kind, decent people who are not capable of hurting each other, except by accident or under extreme provocation. They are sheep.

I mean nothing negative by calling them sheep. To me it is like the pretty, blue robin's egg. Inside it is soft and gooey but someday it will grow into something wonderful. But the egg cannot survive without its hard blue shell. Police officers, soldiers, and other warriors are like that shell, and someday the civilization they protect will grow into something wonderful. For now, though, they need warriors to protect them from the predators.

"Then there are the wolves," the old war veteran said, "and the wolves feed on the sheep without mercy." Do you believe there are wolves out there who will feed on the flock without mercy? You better believe it. There are evil men in this world and they are capable of evil deeds. The moment you forget that or pretend it is not so, you become a sheep. There is no safety in denial.

"Then there are sheepdogs," he went on, "and I'm a sheepdog. I live to protect the flock and confront the wolf."

If you have no capacity for violence then you are a healthy productive citizen, a sheep. If you have a capacity for violence and no empathy for your fellow citizens, then you have defined an aggressive sociopath, a wolf. But what if you have a capacity for violence, and a deep love for your fellow citizens? What do you have then? A sheepdog, a warrior, someone who is walking the hero's path. Someone who can walk into the heart of darkness, into the universal human phobia, and walk out unscathed

Let me expand on this old soldier's excellent model of the sheep, wolves, and sheepdogs. We know that the sheep live in denial, that is what makes them sheep. They do not want to believe that there is evil in the world. They can accept the fact that fires can happen, which is why they want fire extinguishers, fire sprinklers, fire alarms and fire exits throughout their kids' schools.

But many of them are outraged at the idea of putting an armed police officer in their kid's school. Our children are thousands of times more likely to be killed or seriously injured by school violence than fire, but the sheep's only response to the possibility of violence is denial. The idea of someone coming to kill or harm their child is just too hard, and so they chose the path of denial.

The sheep generally do not like the sheepdog. He looks a lot like the wolf. He has fangs and the capacity for violence. The difference, though, is that the sheepdog must not, cannot and will not ever harm the sheep. Any sheep dog who intentionally harms the lowliest little lamb will be punished and removed. The world cannot work any other way, at least not in a representative democracy or a republic such as ours.

Still, the sheepdog disturbs the sheep. He is a constant reminder that there are wolves in the land. They would prefer that he didn't tell them where to go, or give them traffic tickets, or stand at the ready in our airports in camouflage fatigues holding an M-16. The sheep would much rather have the sheepdog cash in his fangs, spray paint himself white, and go, "Baa."

Until the wolf shows up. Then the entire flock tries desperately to hide behind one lonely sheepdog.

The students, the victims, at Columbine High School were big, tough high school students, and under ordinary circumstances they would not have had the time of day for a police officer. They were not bad kids; they just had nothing to say to a cop. When the school was under attack, however, and SWAT teams were clearing the rooms and hallways, the officers had to physically peel those clinging, sobbing kids off of them. This is how the little lambs feel about their sheepdog when the wolf is at the door.

Look at what happened after September 11, 2001 when the wolf pounded hard on the door. Remember how America, more than ever before, felt differently about their law enforcement officers and military personnel? Remember how many times you heard the word 'hero'?

Understand that there is nothing morally superior about being a sheepdog; it is just what you choose to be. Also understand that a sheepdog is a funny critter: He is always sniffing around out on the perimeter, checking the breeze, barking at things that go bump in the night, and yearning for a righteous battle. That is, the young sheepdogs yearn for a righteous battle. The old sheepdogs are a little older and wiser, but they move to the sound of the guns when needed right along with the young ones.

Here is how the sheep and the sheepdog think differently. The sheep pretend the wolf will never come, but the sheepdog lives for that day. After the attacks on September 11, 2001, most of the sheep, that is, most citizens in America said, "Thank God I wasn't on one of those planes." The sheepdogs, the warriors, said, "Dear God, I wish I could have been on one of those planes. Maybe I could have made a difference." When you are truly transformed into a warrior and have truly invested yourself into warriorhood, you want to be there. You want to be able to make a difference.

There is nothing morally superior about the sheepdog--the warrior-- but he does have one real advantage. Only one. And that is that he is able to survive and thrive in an environment that destroys 98 percent of the population.

There is no safety for honest men except by believing all possible evil of evil men. - *Edmund Burke*

When you are done reading this book, we hope that you will have a clear idea that you are either a sheep or a sheepdog. If you determine you are a sheep, go home, kiss the kids good night and sleep like a baby. If it turns out that you are a sheepdog, we hope this book will be your guide to take care of yourself and the sheep you love.

Chapter 1
What This Book Is All About

Have you ever stopped to think how different the world would be without you? How would your family, your friends, or the world in general get along if suddenly your life was wrongfully taken and you were dead?

If you have ever watched the classic movie It's a Wonderful Life, you know these questions were answered for George Bailey.

George openly questioned the value of his life until his Guardian Angel Clarence showed George all the lives he touched and how different his family and his community would be without him. In the movie, George gained a keen perspective of his real value to others (not to mention his value to himself) and how very important he was to those he had touched.

Just like George, your life is precious to yourself and those you touch in too many ways to list here. So close your eyes and pretend you have a guardian angel to take you back in time, and consider for a moment all the different ways the world would forever change if someone wrongfully took your life ten years ago.

What future accomplishments will you never begin? How will your spouse's life be changed?

How different will your children's lives be without you?

Even total strangers who benefit from your life will feel your loss.

I know that your death is not fun to think about but I want you to understand you are important to many people and that the ripple effect of your absence will be huge. So you have a decision to make. To what lengths are you willing to go to be prepared to protect your life for yourself, for those who love you, and those who depend upon you?

This book will help you understand the physical, moral, legal and financial issues and responsibilities that accompany the decision to carry a firearm for your personal protection and those you love.

Carry Laws

A bit of background, first.

There are, to oversimplify just a bit, three kinds of handgun license laws in the United States: "constitutional carry", "shall issue," and "may-issue."

"Constitutional carry" has become the moniker for states that allow its citizens to carry a firearm, openly, and in some states concealed, without any type of license or any type of training. One must be able to lawfully possess a firearm under federal and state laws. Every state that has Constitutional carry has one or more restrictions as to how, when and where a firearm is carried. Since 1872 Wisconsin has always been a constitutionally "open carry" state and also had some restrictions (although fewer now than before passage of Wisconsin's new weapons law. Even though this is the case, until 2009, a person exercising their right to open carry was subject to harassment and arrest by law enforcement. This is an excellent example of that old axiom; rights are like muscles, if you do not use them over time you lose them.

The second category is the "shall-issue" states. Wisconsin is now in this group. In "shall-issue" states, any objectively qualifying adult can get a carry license simply by taking and passing the appropriate training, having their background examined, filling out and filing a form with the issuing authority, and paying a fee. The majority of states have "shall issue" laws.

In "may-issue" states, licenses are issued only at the discretion of the local authorities who are free to deny licenses for any reason, or no reason at all.

In some respects a firearm license is like a driver's license. A driver's license *allows* you to drive a car, but does not *require* you to, and both licenses can be taken away if you violate certain laws.

There is an important distinction between getting a carry license and carrying a handgun in public. Some people do not plan to ever carry a handgun, but may choose to get a carry license anyway. A license gives you the *option* of carrying a handgun. But, just as with a driver's license and driving a car, having a carry license and carrying a handgun is a responsibility you should take very seriously.

For either license you have to train and qualify. There is work involved, and some expense although not a lot, and there should be some careful thought as well.

About the only thing we can promise you when carrying a handgun is: *A gun never solves problems*.

At best, the *lawful* use of a handgun can substitute one set of serious consequences for another. If you have a *defensive gun use* (DGU) in a public place you should expect to be arrested, possibly prosecuted for any one or more of a long list of firearm related crimes, spend a tidy sum of money, and have persistent emotional and possibly even permanent physical injuries. In addition, there will be the instant fame and misfortune of being judged by the court of public opinion about what you did, the way you did it without benefit of the facts. Or, you can be dead. Even if you are found innocent of all criminal charges, there are a host of possible civil lawsuits staring you in the face.

Yes, that is better than being raped, kidnapped, suffer great bodily harm or murdered. But it is better to avoid the whole problem in the first place.

Who this book is for

While there are quite a few very good books on the issues of carrying handguns, *The Wisconsin Guide for Armed Citizens* is different: it is about carrying and using a weapon in *Wisconsin*.

Most of the principles involved apply anywhere; staying alert in Wisconsin is no different than staying alert anywhere else.

But Wisconsin is different from most other "shall issue" states. There are portions of both Wisconsin carry and Wisconsin self-defense laws that leave a person saying, "That just does not make sense." This is probably true for the untrained citizen. Self-defense laws are tricky. They are laws retroactively applied to your situation requiring you to anticipate the future outcome and using your "privileged use of force" to stop the threat. Our goal is to help you understand the laws and how they apply thereby increasing the probability you will avoid serious consequences by making better decisions.

Until the Wisconsin Personal Protection Act - WPPA (the name we have given the law) passed, the concealed carrying of handguns in public by citizens was prohibited in Wisconsin. Many other states have experience with armed citizens carrying weapons in any number of fashions, and understand the whole process of carry training and license issuance. In Wisconsin, authorities have gotten used to the idea of open carrying armed citizens. The new law is the result of years of lobbying and teaching legislators and cajoling the public that armed citizens are perfectly normal. Wisconsin is after all the forty-eighth state to adopt a carry law that was over a decade in the making.

Wisconsin laws are uniquely Wisconsin, just as every other state has their own unique laws. Along with each state's statutes is applicable case law coloring and interpreting how statutes are to be applied. The WPPA did not change the Wisconsin statutes and case law regulating the use or threat of deadly force. Those laws are different, in significant ways, than those of other states. Those who wish to carry in Wisconsin need to know what the laws are in Wisconsin. The opposite is also true. When traveling to other states you must be prepared to follow the applicable laws in that state.

Here is one example: In many states (Minnesota and Missouri, for example) residents may only carry with any license honored by their state. Residents of Wisconsin can open carry without a license. Wisconsin residents may carry a concealed handgun or electronic weapon in his or her own dwelling, place of business, or on land that they own, lease or legally occupy without a license. However, Wisconsin residents desiring to carry a concealed weapon in *public* may only do so with a Wisconsin license.

If you are going to carry a handgun in Wisconsin, you should know the difference between what is common sense and what is legal. It is important to understand that what is now legal may challenge community standards in ways people are not ready to accept. Therefore, a gentle introduction to the "armed citizen" concept may be needed.

If you have been reading the WPPA and wonder what it all means, this book is for you. If you have been wondering what is involved in getting a license and carrying a handgun both in legal and practical terms this book is for you.

If you already have a personal safety concern, a stalker, an abusive ex-spouse, or you work or live in a bad neighborhood this book is for you.

If you are considering taking a job where you may be required to carry a handgun as a citizen this book is for you.

If you are wondering what kind of training and equipment you will need, you will learn that in these pages.

This book is especially for you if you have been wondering about the moral, legal, practical and communal issues involved in using less than lethal or lethal force.

You *do not* need to be an experienced gun owner or have ever held a firearm to benefit from this book. You do not even have to like guns.

If you are an experienced gun owner this book is definitely for you. Many people who have owned guns for most or all of their lives have yet to deal with the laws and mechanics of day-to-day handgun carry.

If you are a police officer wondering whether or not you should be worried about the changes in the law and what it means to you, this book is for you. For now think about this: there are numerous reports of license holders saving police officers' lives. You do not need to worry about license holders: we are the good guys.

Even if you are a passionate gun control advocate and you think all handguns should be banned, this book is for you. You should know about the issues involved as somewhere or sometime you will see or meet an armed citizen. Hopefully this book will help you understand that armed citizens are not a threat to you.

Regardless of how you feel about firearms or people carrying handguns in public there are some changes that have been made and you should know about them.

This book is also for a relatively small number of people who may think that carrying a handgun around in public is fun and cool. The enactment of Wisconsin's license laws *does not* mean that they can now strut around in public, not taking any guff from anybody because they have a gun. We sincerely hope and expect to change the attitudes of those people.

Who we are

LEOSA Trainers, Inc. is dedicated to providing outstanding training in firearms safety, storage, and basic firearms handling, as well as license-to-carry instruction.

For most of his adult life, **Gene German's** profession was a commercial insurance broker, counseling business owners about their business risks, negotiating the transfer of the risks to an insurer and suggested appropriate risk management techniques to manage risks his clients chose to keep.

As president of LEOSA Trainers Inc, Gene applies similar risk management techniques to train instructors and their students to know how to protect themselves from the unexpected threats they may encounter. He has taught citizens in Minnesota, Wisconsin and Illinois how to responsibly carry lethal force in public since 2004.

Gene became a member of the leadership team and served as the Executive Director of Gun Owners Civil Rights Alliance (GOCRA) a Minnesota grassroots Second Amendment advocacy group. GOCRA was instrumental in passing the Minnesota Personal Protection Act (MPPA) in 2003 and for its re-passage in 2005. Gene worked as a registered lobbyist on firearm related issues representing Minnesota's 500,000 firearms owners at the Capitol in St. Paul. Gene has testified before the Minnesota and Wisconsin legislatures on several occasions concerning carry laws.

Gene founded the Wisconsin Patriots in 2007 with the goals of reestablishing unlicensed open carry also known as "Constitutional Carry" as lawful in Wisconsin (accomplished in 2009) and to enact a good carry law. Gene proposed a "dual system" to legislators preserving unlicensed open carry and adding a carry license with fewer restrictions for those who would agree to be trained and have their good character verified. The legislature and governor embraced his ideas and a "dual system" was enacted in 2011.

Gene and Tim Grant wrote Wisconsin's first constitutional carry course in 2009, and the Wisconsin License to Carry course. Gene is also the co-author with Tim Grant of the *Minnesota Guide for Armed Citizens*, and the *Illinois Guide for Armed Citizens*.

In 2012, Gene founded LEOSA Trainers, Inc. (LTI) to provide the training necessary for retired and separated law enforcement officers who reside in Minnesota and wish to carry a firearm nationwide. Gene designed LTI's training to be much more than just administering a shooting qualification. LTI offers a unique combination of Minnesota carry training and LEOSA training to clients who desire both. LTI's training also includes how a client could properly insure themselves for a defensive gun use so their life savings does not have to be at risk in retirement.

Gene formally resigned his positions as Wisconsin and Illinois NACFI state director, and severed LTI's partnership with NACFI in August of 2014. This decision was necessary to enable him to provide continued support for LTI's instructors and to devote his time on expanding LTI's permit to carry training business in Minnesota, Wisconsin and Illinois.

Tim Fleming Grant, President of NACFI, is a political activist and marketing professional. Grant's interest in firearms and self defense began in February of 1996 when his cousin was killed in a drive-by shooting in Golden Valley, Minnesota. After four years of committed part-time work on the leadership team of Concealed Carry Reform, Now!, Grant left his position as National Sales Manager for a division of Norstan and later, Siemens to focus more time on changing Minnesota's carry laws. As CCRN's lead strategic planner and elections manager, Grant played a key role in developing and guiding the Minnesota Personal Protection Act through the Minnesota Legislature. Grant holds an MBA from the University of St. Thomas, graduate credits from St. Paul Seminary and a Bachelor of Arts degree in Political Science and Economics from the University of Minnesota. He also holds both Instructor and Certifier ratings from NACFI.

Orientation

When developing LEOSA Trainers, Inc. training courses, the requisite books and the student materials, we did a lot of reading and research. One of the things we found irritating about much of the writing on handgun self-defense is that many authors assumed their audience possessed a lot of familiarity with the issues and with firearms.

Transportation and cars are not only for roadway design engineers, mechanics, and automotive hobbyists; medical care is not just for doctors and nurses; and self-defense and personal safety are not just for law enforcement officers, security and body guards, or even the secret service. Maintaining one's personal constant state of peace is for everyone. Wisconsin's new carry law redefines how one maintains their constant state of peace.

Whether or not you should apply for a carry license has a lot more to do with your own personality, morality, and situation than it does with whether or not you know or want to know a lot about firearms. A carry license is not a necessary accessory for a firearms hobbyist. On the contrary, it is entirely reasonable to have no interest at all in firearms beyond personal protection and choose to obtain a carry license.

Our counsel is based on a wealth of experience and is focused toward people new to carrying of handguns. We have nothing against other legitimate uses of guns for hunting, target shooting or other recreational purposes. LEOSA Trainers, Inc. training courses and this book are about the day-to-day and emergency issues of people carrying handguns, *in Wisconsin* for personal protection. That is an important distinction.

Even people who have owned guns for many years may never have carried one in public on a daily basis. They have not had to think through the many issues involved in carrying a handgun, from routine encounters with police to the thankfully rare situations where a handgun must be drawn in public.

Far too many people, including some who have owned guns all of their lives, have picked up a lot of misinformation from television and newspapers. Few have the correct understanding about the laws involving self-defense or practical matters involving carrying of a handgun as an armed citizen.

That is what this book is all about.

A handgun and a fire extinguisher

Thankfully the vast majority of people who carry a handgun will never have a defensive gun use. Coincidentally, those people who wisely own a fire extinguisher hope they never have to use it either.

When you buy fire a extinguisher you hope and expect that you will never have to use it, but you also know that, should your home catch fire, a convenient fire extinguisher may make what could have been a horrible incident a lot less horrible. A fire extinguisher is only one of the things a prudent homeowner buys in order to protect themselves and the family: smoke detectors and good locks are every bit as important.

And so it is with handguns. They are purchased and often times carried in case of a life threatening attack. Random acts of violence occur randomly so a handgun, a defensive weapon, needs to be readily available all the time. Being caught without a handgun when a random attack finds you is something no one wants to experience.

Humor

Carrying a handgun in public is a serious matter, and must be taken seriously. That does not mean that a little humor every now and then is a bad idea, in fact, we think it is essential. We hope that the occasional touches of humor in this book will be appreciated.

There are, however, things we do not consider funny. Joking about pointing a gun at another human being or carelessly handling your firearms are acts that diminish all armed citizens. It is your responsibility to make a positive impression.

Keeping it simple

We believe in keeping things simple whenever possible. There are sound psychological, legal, and physiological reasons for this when it comes to life-threatening encounters initiating a defensive gun use.

However, some topics cannot be oversimplified. The law and its application are complicated. We have synthesized many of the legal concepts to universally applicable formulas to assist you when making split second life and death decisions.

What a license changes

Before you decide whether or not to take training and apply for a carry license, please understand what it changes. Legally speaking, it changes one thing and one thing only: *a carry license allows you to carry a handgun in public in some situations or places where it would otherwise be unlawful to do so.*

It does not change the law of self-defense in or out of the home. It does not change whether or not you are allowed to own firearms. It does not change the laws involved in storing handguns at home or at your place of business. It does not make it suddenly legal for convicted criminals to carry firearms. *Most importantly is does not give anyone the right to just shoot someone!*

The chart that follows covers a majority of the situations involving carrying of a firearm.

Rights	Non license holders	License Holders
Owning firearms	Yes	Yes
Carrying loaded/unloaded firearms at home	Yes	Yes
Carrying loaded/unloaded firearms at place of business	Yes	Yes
Carrying firearms, unloaded, in a case, in the trunk of the car	Yes	Yes
Use of lethal force in self-defense	Yes	Yes
Carrying a firearm into school zones	No	Yes
Carrying a firearm in most public places	Yes	Yes
Carrying a loaded firearm in the passenger compartment of a car	Yes	Yes
Carrying firearms onto schools grounds (K-12)	No	No
Acting as a police officer	No	No

The important thing a license changes is the right to carry a handgun in public.

It is not a "junior G-man badge."

It does not change the legal right people have to defend themselves under Wisconsin law.

To repeat, the *only* important thing it changes, legally, is the right to carry a firearm in public.

Although we are offering a great deal of sound advice, we are not offering formal legal advice. For that, you should consult an attorney.

And remember: a gun never solves problems.

CHAPTER 2
Why Would Anybody Want a Carry License?

Across the United States, millions of people in forty eight states have handgun carry licenses.

The reasons vary as much as the people do.

Some have them because they need to be able to carry a firearm in order to protect other people or other people's money, bank guards for example. Some people have licenses in order to protect their own assets. Many license holders are small business owners who want to protect both their bank deposits and themselves during the sometimes-harrowing trip to the bank at the end of the day. In rural areas, in many states, some people have carry licenses because it enables them to lawfully keep their firearms in the passenger compartment of the car or truck, rather than locked in the trunk.

Most people who have carry licenses have them for personal protection. Some are worried about a specific threat, such as a stalker or an abusive ex-spouse. Others are in risky jobs, such as convenience store clerks, pizza delivery drivers, and cab drivers. A few just have them to exercise their right to be their own first responder.

People who *carry* guns lawfully are far less likely to be victims of violent crime. We emphasize carry. Most armed citizens do not appear as easy victims to the bad guys. Their demeanor, the way they carry themselves, and the level of situational awareness they project convinces the bad guys into looking for a softer target. Armed citizens present themselves this way because they are armed. Whether the bad guy sees the gun or not is irrelevant. He will know that you are not a soft target. Carrying the gun is the easy part. Ever having to use it is the hard part. That is where solid training pays off.

Out experience shows us that many people who have carry licenses do not regularly carry a handgun in public. Their reasons vary widely.

One of the few universal truths about a handgun is that it never gets lighter as the day goes by. Defensive gun uses are low frequency high consequence events. Licenses holders who do not regularly carry their handgun are betting on "low frequency" to mean "zero." A handgun is useful if the rare life-threatening situation confronts you, unless you have left it at home.

The burden of carrying a handgun is not carrying it. It is your responsibility, both for moral and legal reasons, to maintain control of your handgun. Leaving a handgun unattended is only looking for trouble.

There are other issues. Wisconsin law allows the Department of Justice to issue licenses to carry a handgun. For the majority of armed citizens this means concealing the handgun. For personal, situational and communal reasons armed citizens value this form of carry. Exposing the handgun can not only startle people, but can also result in the police being summoned to a "man with a gun" call. That can be not only annoying, but potentially dangerous.

The problems do not stop there.

People carrying handguns have to remember they are armed. This may sound odd, but it can be like forgetting you put your glasses on you head. While it may be illegal to take a pair of nail scissors through the security checkpoint at an airport, somebody who forgets he has one of those items really does not have anything to worry about beyond losing it. A license holder who forgets that he or she has a handgun at the checkpoint *will* have some serious explaining to do. In Wisconsin, a license holder going to pick up his or her children at school has to remember to stay off school property. The firearm must be secured and the vehicle parked on the street before entering school property.

"I forgot" is not a legal defense.

Even ordinary social situations can become difficult at times.

Take drinking, for example. Wisconsin law allows license holders to carry in bars. This is because guns do not drink. The law does not allow an armed citizen to consume alcohol either. Should a license holder desire a couple of cocktails, the best solution is unloading and storing the firearm in a case as one would do if transporting or store it at home before hitting the bars.

As you have read many reasons for not carrying exist. So why would any reasonable person ever want to?

It is simple. On those rare occasions when a handgun is necessary in self-defense, there is no good substitute.

Less than lethal options, like electronic control devices, billy clubs, or purses require an attacker to get very close, and often do not work well against an armed attacker. Karate and other martial arts training are fine in theory but, in practice, they are useful for only the most proficient and fit practitioners. Improvised weapons like car keys or a heavy flashlight are not effective substitutes for a gun.

Statistically, the single most effective way to deter or stop a determined attacker is to produce a handgun and be prepared to use it. Fortunately, for the attacker, they can decide to flee before being shot by their intended victim. It is better for everyone if the attacker leaves the scene rather than engaging the victim in a fight the attacker is most likely to lose, and lose big. Despite surviving the attack many victims suffer some physical injury before they can stop the attacker.

More generally armed citizens have a positive effect on the overall crime rates. John Lott's studies have shown that when enough people take out licenses it lowers violent crime rates. This phenomenon is called the "halo effect" and shows up when at least 1% of the state's population is perceived to be lawfully armed.

Research by criminologists confirms what is happening is that criminals are responding to information about their own risk.[1] The fact that there may be armed citizens present, either as the criminal's would-be

---

[1] *Armed and Dangerous*, by James D. Write and Peter H. Rossi (Aldine de Gruyter: New York; ISBN 0-202-30331-4), was the result of a study of over 2,000 convicted felons. Of these, two-thirds admitted having been "scared off, shot at, wounded, or captured by an armed victim," and two-fifths of them had decided not to commit a crime because they knew or believed that their intended victim was armed.

victim or as bystanders persuades some career criminals to make different choices because of their increased perception of risk to themselves. Of the thousands of law-enforcement officers (LEOs) in Wisconsin, at best 30% (2,100) are on duty at any given time. Criminals having to also worry about 200,000 lawfully armed citizens increases a violent criminal's chance of a bad result by about 95 times. An attacker may decide to move to a different locale where the risk of being shot is less or switch to breaking into unoccupied cars. The abusive ex-spouse may worry more about the possibility of being shot while trying to beat up his or her ex than the consequences of violating an Order for Protection.

Regardless of *why* "shall-issue" laws lower violent crime, the important point is that they do.

We know that license issuance is a good thing for society in general because of its effect on violent crime and for ordinary day-to-day civility. As Robert A. Heinlein wrote, "an armed society is a polite society." Heinlein was writing about fictional societies. Still, incidents of lawfully armed citizens behaving badly are nearly impossible to find. Conversely, it is possible that the presence of armed citizens have caused some loud and rude people to behave better in public.

No license holder should ever do anything to encourage being feared by the community. The old axiom, "don't do anything to scare the women or the horses" may be a little dated and sexist, but still has a ring of truth. As you will see, when you carry a handgun, you must take more precautions to avoid confrontations that could escalate.

Getting a carry license because of a safety concern

In many other states it is at least theoretically possible to get a carry license issued within hours because of an immediate threat.

It makes much more sense to get a carry license in advance of a known threat and then make day-to-day decisions regarding carrying should a threatening situation appear.

This will be discussed in more detail in a later chapter, but it is important to note that while carrying a handgun may be an important part of personal protection it is *not* the only part of it. Those people who have specific personal safety concerns such as: a stalker, a physically abusive relationship, a criminal one may be testifying against in court, should consult their attorney, the local police and other safety professionals as to what else you should do. A temporary restraining order or the equivalent order is not terribly difficult to get. While it is just a piece of paper of questionable affect, it can be very useful in dealing with the police if summoned.

Why somebody would not want to have a carry license

It is simply a fact that the majority of eligible citizens will not get a carry license. They are sheep! There are both good reasons and bad reasons why somebody would not want to take out a carry license, or even own a firearm for self-defense at all. Let us look at a few.

"My gun might be taken away and used against me"

That is a very serious problem for police officers. Fourteen percent of police officers who are killed are shot with their own firearms. Police have very different exposure to that sort of threat than citizens do. They carry their firearms openly, and they frequently come into close contact with criminals, often needing to fight with them in order to subdue and arrest them. That is something an armed citizen should never find themselves doing because you are not a licensed peace officer.

The notion of citizens drawing guns in self-defense and having their own gun turned on them is an urban myth. It happens on TV shows a lot, but in real life not so much. It is difficult to find an instance of a citizen being disarmed. This is understandable; when an attacker is confronted by an armed citizen most of the time he flees.

"There are all those accidental gun deaths"

Every fatality, no matter what the cause, is tragic. But realistically firearms are among the *least* common causes of accidental fatalities in the United States. The National Safety Council, a nonpartisan organization, consistently reports fewer than a thousand accidental firearms deaths per year, or about a fourth as many as drownings, and about the same number as deaths from falling out of bed. Over the twenty years that the NSC has been measuring causes of accidental death, gun accidents have been an almost invisible cause, and the number has dropped, despite the increase in both the population and the number of guns owned in the United States.

Most firearm accidents in the United States are hunting accidents, but the number is consistently dropping due to youth hunter safety courses. It is not a good idea to take gun safety casually. If you make a habit of always following the basic rules of firearms safety, your chances of accidentally or negligently injuring, much less killing, yourself or somebody else is zero.

Safety is no accident.

"Guns are a lousy way to settle personal disputes"

This is *absolutely* correct.

Guns are not just a lousy way to settle a dispute, they are an *illegal* way to settle *any kind* of dispute. The only legally justifiable reason to point a gun at another human being is because of a reasonable fear of an imminent threat of death or great bodily harm. Using guns to settle heated arguments with family, neighbors, or strangers is not just unlawful, but it is also rare, at least among license holders.

Of the millions of license holders across the nation, it is almost impossible to find one who has used a firearm in an irresponsible way.

Beyond the bad reasons

The main reason most eligible people do not get carry license is that they cannot use a gun defensively. They have the mistaken belief that someone else (the police) will always be there to save them. We believe becoming an armed citizen is beneficial to you and your family. It is a very personal decision only you can make. Active decision making about a carry license is the only way to learn about its benefits, responsibilities, and your capabilities. Not considering a carry license is the "bad reason."

A few people may believe they are incapable of controlling their temper and dare not provide themselves easy access to a tool that can do a lot of damage in one uncontrolled moment. We think they are making a good choice.

It may come as a surprise that approximately 20% of students taking a license to carry training class do not apply for a license. Once the responsibilities and gravity of the split second decisions that are required when applying lethal force are understood a license to carry is something they decide against.

At least make an informed decision!

Is it right for you?

No one can decide that for you. We can say that qualifying for and getting a carry license does give you some options.

Getting a license to carry, carrying a firearm and using a firearm are three entirely different issues. Before ever applying for a carry license some soul searching must be done. Do you just want to carry a firearm, or are you capable and prepared to use it? The choice of being able to use lethal force including shooting an attacker is a individual and very personal decision. Your soul search will include your upbringing, religious training, and personal set of moral values. Along with training you will be better prepared to make an informed decision.

Most people will get a license to carry in advance of a real threat. It is done to be prepared.

Our recommendation is to read about it and think about it. If you decide a license is right for you, take a training course from LEOSA Trainers, Inc., or other high quality training organization.

And remember: a gun never solves problems.

CHAPTER 3
Staying Out of Trouble

The most important thing for a license holder to do is to stay out of trouble in the first place.

The advantages of this are obvious: a violent confrontation that you avoid will not get you injured, killed, prosecuted, or sued. Many people who have survived lethal confrontations, even if they manage to avoid being injured themselves suffer from a variety of psychological affects, depression, anxiety, Post-Traumatic Stress Disorder, etc.

On television the effects are usually understated or solved just before the last commercial. That is fine in fiction, but that is not the way it works in real life.

Even when lethal force is justified legally, morally, and tactically there are serious important and lasting consequences. Using lethal force even when entirely legal, has negative effects on everybody involved. Those who defend themselves against violent attack are still victims. They are just "victims of a different type."

Bob, not his real name, shot and killed a robber in his store twenty years ago. The Grand Jury returned a "no bill." They said there was not any reason to believe that he might be guilty of a crime. Twenty years later he still takes drugs for depression and anxiety.

Being involved in a defensive gun use is an awful thing, and going to some trouble to avoid it is a good idea for everybody, particularly those who choose to carry handguns in public.

Your four tactical options

In every situation you will have four tactical options when assessing a situation.

For our purposes I will define "a threat" as: 1) someone who you did not provoke, 2) who has somehow convinced you that they have the capability and the intent to do you great bodily harm or to murder you.

Each tactical option will be dictated by circumstances over which you have no control. The specific situation you are facing at the moment will determine which options are available, and they will change as the event unfolds before you. Maintaining your "situational awareness" will help you to recognize when new options become available to you that may not have been practical just moments before. Your decision of which option to use, stop using or when to do something else entirely will change during the course of the attack.

Each option may be both scalable and/or reversible. Being scalable means you can increase or decrease the action you are taking. For example, if you decide to leave, you could walk slowly or run as fast as possible. By reversible I mean that if you take this action, can you stop doing it or reverse it. So, let's say you left, unless you have a very good reason, perhaps your grandchild did not make it out with you, you would not return once you were safe outside.

Tactical options flow in the same way that escalation of force does. It begins with the most minimum of options and escalates from there. Tactical options are not the same thing as the legal conditions or what I call "elements" that are needed to legally use lethal force in defense of yourself or others. For example it could be totally legal to shoot someone, but tactically your shooting would be a disaster because you would cause more harm to innocent bystanders.

Your first option is to do nothing.
You may choose to elect not to take any action at all and just observe what is going on in front of you. You are considering your options. You are collecting data. So you are very busy "doing nothing" as you are

doing nothing. To the extent that you are paying more or less attention to the situation "doing nothing" is scalable. Doing nothing is reversible because you can decide to do something when the opportunity presents itself.

Your second option is to leave if it is safe and practical.

When a situation makes you uncomfortable, the best thing to do might be to leave before any trouble starts. By practicing situational awareness you should know where the available exits are when you enter a room. If you are with other people can you manage to get everyone in your party out safely with you? If the level of threat is too high for you and your party to exit, you may need to wait until an opportunity to leave presents itself. Leaving is scalable depending upon the situation, because you can move from one point of cover to another or perhaps walk or run to the exit. If you are able to leave if the threat is still present inside, leaving should not be reversible without a very good reason to do so (your spouse did not make it out with you). Once you are safe, there is no point in getting your gun from your vehicle for example, and going back into harm's way.

Your third option is to use less than lethal force.

Your less than lethal force actions may be anything from issuing a loud and stern verbal command to drop the weapon, to taking physical actions such as striking or shoving an attacker. Think of it this way, if you did not have a gun with you, what you would be doing and do that. Less than lethal force is scalable because you can increase or decrease the level of force you have taken. This option is reversible, because if it worked you can stop applying force and if it didn't work, you can escalate to lethal force.

Your fourth option is to use lethal force.

This begins with the threat of lethal force or drawing your gun from its holster, and includes firing your handgun or using any other type of force that could reasonably be expected to cause death or great bodily harm. Lethal force is scalable. You can shoot one, two, three or more times, but only as many shots as it takes to stop the threat. Every magazine has a bullet in it that goes from reasonable force to excessive force. When you get to the last reasonable force bullet, you must stop shooting or you have used excessive force which is a crime.

Lethal force is reversible. It is reversible until the moment you pull the trigger and shoot. After a bullet has left the gun, there is no taking the bullet back.

Situational awareness

The key to avoiding problems is maintaining a reasonable level of alertness or situational awareness. This is particularly true for avoiding street crimes like mugging, assault, robbery, and rape. Being situationally aware has two advantages: it helps you avoid trouble, and appearing to be alert helps to persuade trouble to avoid you. Generally speaking, criminals are opportunists. As trainer Clint Smith puts it, "If you look like prey, you will be eaten."

When you are unaware of your surroundings and any possible threat for example, when you are asleep, it would take some serious effort to gain your attention. Being "unaware" is necessary to sleep, and should also be OK, at home with the doors locked watching TV. By being unaware of your surrounding, any unusual disturbance may cause a startle reflex.

The next level of situation awareness is when you have a deliberate awareness of your surroundings and make it a habit to pay attention to what is going on around you. You are calm, relaxed, and not concerned about an immediate threat, but looking for things out of the ordinary. When you are waiting at a bus stop, you watch the folks around you, rather than burying yourself in a newspaper or a book. When you are driving you make it a habit to look in the rear-view mirror and notice if you are being followed. It is not a matter of making major changes in how you live your life: it is a matter of being constantly aware of what is going on around you and how people are acting.

It is a good idea to make a habit of staying this alert whenever you are out in public. It is not just a matter of personal safety although awareness is the key to that. Life is just more interesting when you are paying attention to what is going on around you.

The next level is when you have identified a possible threat based upon their capability and intent to hurt you. It is time to consider your tactical options. If others are with you, a plan to get them out of harms way is required. If you do not have a plan for this eventuality you should create one. Perhaps have a secret word or phrase such as "rockcut" or "go check the dog" to alert family member what to do to temporarily create separation from you and to call the police.

The good news is the situation is either going to improve or continue to get worst. If it gets worse your mind-set needs to move to one of "I am going to survive" by fighting for my life. Because you are under attack you have to protect yourself by any reasonable means. Should an opportunity to retreat or leave presents itself, take it. When you are safe, call for help including medical assistance if needed then find your family.

We will discuss all of the physiological and psychological implications later. For now, the best time to figure out how to handle a problem is before it happens. Think about "what if" scenarios when you are going about your day. What if I was attacked right now? What are my options? When under attack, you will go into survival mode and revert to how you have trained. Practicing "what if" is a basic form of training.

Avoiding conflict

"Alternative Means of Conflict Resolution" can be looked at as a fancy way of saying, "Do not escalate an argument into a fight." It is a good idea to cultivate a thick skin if you are carrying a handgun. It is important to avoid conflict because any conflict you are involved in automatically is escalated to the level of an armed conflict. This is true if for no other reason; you are armed even if the other person is not. How police respond to an armed conflict is considerable more dangerous for everybody than their response to an unarmed conflict.

You are an armed citizen who has just been involved in a fender-bender. Some idiot has just backed into you, damaging your new car. You are understandably annoyed and the other person is equally upset. The temptation is to leap out of your car and go shout at the other driver. Understandable, yes, but not a good idea. He or she starts shouting at you. You must resist the temptation to shout back. Stay calm and aware and call the police. You are armed. At this point your responsibility is to be civil and to not escalate the argument into a confrontation. This is good advice for everybody, but it is even more important for armed citizens. In the next chapter we will explain why this is so important.

You should be in Condition Orange and constantly evaluating the situation. Is the idiot just blowing off steam by shouting and swearing, or does he intend to attack you? Can you calm him down with words or perhaps it is better to let him shout for awhile? In any case, staying alert and avoiding escalation is the first best option.

Carrying a firearm changes everything. Your reactions must be lawful. In this case that greatly limits your options. This would be a good time to recall the four options discussed on page 20. Consider each and how it may play out so you can chose the best one.

One thing is for sure. Drawing your handgun is not an available option at this time.

The proper conclusion to this incident is for the police to show up, hand you accident report forms, see that you exchange pertinent information and you each go your separate ways.

Congratulations, you just demonstrated that an armed society is a polite society!

Being aware of what is going on around you, being situationally aware to avoid trouble is a three-step approach:

1. Be nice. If you must have an unpleasant discussion with somebody, do it later over the phone.
2. If you see something suspicious, avoid it.
3. Just because you are armed, you are not going to go places you know are dangerous.

Avoid the conflict, and avoid the consequences

And remember: a gun never solves problems.

CHAPTER 4
Lethal Force, in Law and Practice

First of all, relax. You are not going to be buried with a lot of legal jargon in this chapter. However, when it comes to the lawful use of force, there is just no way around getting into some of the nitty-gritty of the legalities and we have to deal with those.

This book is intended to be a general discussion of the judicious use of force for self–defense and the affirmative self-defense law in Wisconsin. We also discuss the law associated with a Wisconsin Carry license. While this book was written with the help of from some very experienced local attorneys, the author is not a Wisconsin attorney and cannot give you specific legal advice. That is the job of your attorney.

The law is never simple. Even when principles are clear and well-developed the exact facts of each situation (at every moment, even as they change) can cause the legal answer to vary as tiny changes occur. This book discusses principles. Only your own legal counsel, armed with the specifics of the law and the facts of your own situation can give you "legal advice" that you can depend on.

You will notice that court cases are cited. Statutory law is colored over time by judicial rulings. How a specific ruling affects the application of a specific law can be very important. This book and the discussion of legal principles therein, take into account judicial rulings and jury instructions that may apply.

It is important for you to know that Wisconsin is a "preemption state." This means that, with very few exceptions, the State legislature has absolute control over the regulation of firearms and their use. The laws and case law we are going to discuss here and later in the book apply border-to-border. No local unit of government can enforce or enact an ordinance or resolution unless it is the same as or similar to or no more stringent than a state statute. Preemption also means that a local unit of government cannot create ordinances or resolutions to regulate that which the state does not regulate. For example, open carry, also called constitutional carry, has always been legal. It has never been prohibited by the legislature. Local units of government have repeatedly attempted to make it illegal. Preemption has kept them from being able to do so.

Most ordinary, law-abiding citizens, go through their entire life without ending up in a criminal court either as a defendant or as a witness testifying against an attacker. If you do your best to avoid trouble and are successful, you will never have to convince a jury why you should not be sent to prison. We are talking "high consequences" here.

Self-defense

The possession of a carry license does not change Wisconsin law about the use of force one way or the other.

Wisconsin law uses the concept of "privilege." Self-defense is only one of six circumstances that can be claimed as privileged. The fact that the armed citizen's conduct is privileged, although otherwise criminal, is a defense to prosecution of any crime based on that conduct. The defense of privilege can be claimed under any one of the six following circumstances. (Wis. Stat. 939.45)

(1)   When the actor's [armed citizen] conduct occurs under circumstances of coercion or necessity so as to be privileged (Wis. Stat.939.48 or 939.49). (Wis.stat 939.45(1))

"Coercion" is threat by an attacker causing the victim to reasonably believe that the only means to prevent death or great bodily harm to themselves or others is to cooperate and carry out the orders of the attacker. (Wis. Stat. 939.46(1))

"Necessity" is pressure of natural physical forces which causes the actor [armed citizen] reasonably to believe that his or her act is the only means of preventing imminent public disaster, or imminent death or great bodily harm to the actor or another and which causes him or her so to act, is a defense to a prosecution for any crime based on that act. (Wis. Stat. 939.47)

(2)   When the actor's [armed citizen] conduct is in defense of persons or property under any of the circumstances described (Wis. Stat.939.48 or 939.49). (Wis.stat 939.45(2)).

Number 2 above is the foundation of Wisconsin self-defense law which is as follows:

A person [armed citizen] is privileged to threaten or intentionally use force against another for the purpose of preventing or terminating what the person reasonably believes to be an unlawful interference with his or her person by such other person (attacker). The actor [armed citizen] may intentionally use only such force or threat thereof as the actor [armed citizen] reasonably believes is necessary to prevent or terminate the interference. The actor [armed citizen] may not intentionally use force which is intended or likely to cause death or great bodily harm unless the actor [armed citizen] reasonably believes that such force is necessary to prevent imminent death or great bodily harm to himself or herself. (Wis. Stat. 938.48)

Courts determined in *State v. Camacho* (176 Wis. 2d 860 (1993)) that an imperfect self-defense contains an initial threshold element requirement of a reasonable belief that the defendant was terminating an unlawful interference with his or her person.

A person is privileged to threaten or intentionally use force against another for the purpose of preventing or terminating what the person reasonably believes to be an unlawful interference with the person's property. Only such degree of force or threat thereof may intentionally be used as the actor reasonably believes is necessary to prevent or terminate the interference. It is not reasonable to intentionally use force intended or likely to cause death or great bodily harm for the sole purpose of defense of one's property. (Wis. Stat. 938.49(1))

A person is privileged to defend a 3rd person's property from real or apparent unlawful interference by another under the same conditions and by the same means as those under and by which the person is privileged to defend his or her own property from real or apparent unlawful interference, provided that the person reasonably believes that the facts are such as would give the 3rd person the privilege to defend his or her own property, that his or her intervention is necessary for the protection of the 3rd person's property, and that the 3rd person whose property the person is protecting is a member of his or her immediate family or household or a person whose property the person has a legal duty to protect, or is a merchant and the actor is the merchant's employee or agent. An official or adult employee or agent of a library is privileged to defend the property of the library in the manner specified in this subsection. (Wis. stat. 939.49(2)) (176 Wis. 2d 860 (1993))

Note that defense of property is limited to the use of less than lethal force. Property protection has limitations whose property a 3rd person may protect. Generally, you may only protect property over which you have care, custody, or control. This is based on the relationship you have with the owner of the property.

(3)   When the actor's [armed citizen] conduct is in good faith and is an apparently authorized and reasonable fulfillment of any duties of a public office. (Wis. Stat. 939.45(3))

(4) When the actor's [armed citizen] conduct is a reasonable accomplishment of a lawful arrest. (Wis. Stat. 939.45(4))

Armed citizens should not attempt a citizen's arrest without a clear legal basis supporting the action. Doing so may leave one open to any of a number of other crimes or civil suits.

(5) The fifth defense of privilege deals with the welfare of children and what is or is not an acceptable level of force in punishing a child. (Wis. Stat. 939.45(5)(a) and (b))

(6) When for any other reason the actor's [armed citizen] conduct is privileged by the statutory or common law of this state. (Wis. Stat. 939.45(6))

The sixth defense of privilege is very important for those involved in a DGU. It incorporates excusable homicide by accident or misfortune.

Accident is a defense that negates intent. If a person kills another by accident, the killing could not have been intentional. If used as a defense, accident must be disproved beyond a reasonable doubt.

An armed citizen may demonstrate that he or she was acting lawfully, a necessary element of an accident defense, by showing that he or she was acting in lawful self-defense. For example, if a bystander was injured or killed in the course of a lawful DGU that injury or death should be privileged as accidental. Although intentionally pointing a firearm at another constitutes a violation of Wis. Stat. 941.20, under Wis Stat. 939.48 (1) a person is privileged to point a gun at another person in self-defense if the person reasonably believes that the threat of force is necessary to prevent or terminate what he or she reasonably believes to be an unlawful interference.

Defense of others

Defense of others requires the same circumstances and privilege as to protect oneself. There is however, one big hurdle to cover before coming to the defense of another. You must be psychic! To meet a prosecutor's challenge to the defense a third person, the armed citizen, must have complete knowledge and understanding of the victim's condition (how they came to this place, at this time and in this situation) and state of mind. Being able to articulate how another person feels and what that person is thinking (along with what the attacker is thinking) is for practical purposes impossible. In addition, the armed citizen would need to know the relationship between what is believed to be a victim and an attacker.

As an intervener into a situation, the armed citizen is perceived as another threat to both the attacker and the victim. Your intent is not known, therefore, you are going to be considered a danger to all involved in the incident. This misunderstanding alone can get you killed. Oh, and did I mention, that one of the original parties to the situation is an undercover police officer attempting to make an arrest. Before becoming the third person involved, consider your four options carefully. A situation like this can snowball very quickly into a gunfight and the line between who the good guy and bad guy is will get very blurry very quickly if not bloody. This is what cell phones are for, call the authorities and take mental notes.

One more consideration, you, do not have to do anything. Nothing. There is no law requiring you to act or put yourself in harm's way. One LEOSA Trainers, Inc. instructor comments that "if the victim is not willing to take the steps necessary to learn how to defend themselves, why would they expect me to risk my life to save them." It may sound harsh, but is true.

"Harm" defined

"Great bodily harm" means bodily injury which creates a substantial risk of death, or which causes serious permanent disfigurement, or which causes a permanent or protracted loss or impairment of the function of any bodily member or organ or other serious bodily injury. (Wis. Stat. 939.22)

"Substantial bodily harm" means bodily injury that causes a laceration that requires stitches, staples, or a tissue adhesive; any fracture of a bone; a broken nose; a burn; a petechia; a temporary loss of consciousness, sight or hearing; a concussion; or a loss or fracture of a tooth.

"Bodily Harm" means physical pain or injury, illness, or any impairment of physical condition.

These are the definitions of "harm". How they are applied depends on the individual. For example, someone with a heart condition may reach the risk of great bodily harm more quickly than a healthy individual.

The four elements

This may all seem very confusing. Armed citizens must learn how to take backward looking laws and apply them in a forward thinking fashion. Law is generally written to overlay upon a particular set of historical circumstances to determine if what happened was lawful. Armed citizens have split seconds to apply a set of laws to what they reasonably believe is an imminent event. The question is, *am I within privilege if I take these actions right now?*

This requires a systematic method for quickly assessing the situation, deciding on a course of action, and taking the action. Below is a process to help you through the assessment, decision, and action cycle while under extreme time constraints and stress. They are called the four elements.

For privilege of self-defense to apply, all four elements must be present. The moment any one of the elements is no longer present, the privilege of self-defense also ceases. What privileged actions just a moment before were now criminal. We cannot overstate that all four elements must be present for the entire time you are acting under the privilege of self-defense.

1. Reluctant participant

You cannot be the aggressor in the situation. The situation must be occasioned or developed through no fault of the armed citizen. You cannot provoke an attack with unlawful conduct, and then claim the privilege of self defense.

The privilege lost by provocation may be regained if the armed citizen in good faith withdraws from the fight and gives adequate notice thereof to his or her attacker. The louder and more public your notice is the better.

The best example of a reluctant participant is the run of the mill mugging victim. A person just walking down the street minding their own business and is suddenly confronted by one or more attackers seeking either money or to cause injury.

The practice of avoiding conflict and situational awareness will go a long way in establishing your meeting the reluctant participant requirement. Being able to articulate and support the status of reluctant participant is critical to claim the privilege of self-defense. This is the first link of the self-defense claim that must be present.

2. Reasonably believing that one is in imminent danger of death or great bodily harm

This element has a number of characteristics to be considered.

The first is "reasonably."

Courts have determined "reasonableness" to mean a person's belief is judged from the position of a person of ordinary intelligence and prudence placed in the same situation as the defendant, not a person identical to the defendant placed in the same situation. This is the "reasonable man" test courts must use to create an objective standard to guide the jury's assessment of the actions of the defendant.

In believing something, a person takes the information available and processes it against their life experience, knowledge and training. Believing any given set of circumstances or conditions will not be the same for each person. Even when the facts are the same, believing that one is in imminent danger will probably be different for each person because they will process the information they perceived differently. Additionally, this process is going to take place under a great deal of stress that will affect one's ability to think rationally. The court will allow you to use only that information that contributed to your decision to use lethal force. Anything learned about your attacker after the gun goes bang was not a part of your decision to pull the trigger and will not be considered.

Because this element has many subjective attributes, making a black or white case can be difficult. Gray does exist so it is very important you clearly articulate your belief of the threat. Convincing the court your decisions and actions were justified is what matters.

A determination as to the threat being "imminent" must be made. Imminent is something that is about to occur, impending or likely to occur at any moment. By contrast, this differs from immediate which is occurring without delay, having no time intervening, or the next thing about to happen. For example, an attacker may pose an imminent danger even if he is not at that very moment pointing a weapon at you. Imminent is a broader standard, providing additional time for the armed citizen to make good decisions and take proper actions and to stay out of prison.

Death may seem an obvious condition. However, it is not quite that simple. All people die for the same reason: lack of oxygen to the brain. How the brain became starved of oxygen can vary greatly. This may not provide any insight into how one determines if death is imminent, but does provide a definition for clarification.

As with the first element, having a belief of imminent death or great bodily harm must be present the entire time to claim the privilege of self-defense. The claim is only valid until the threat has ceased. When the threat ceases because of something you did or for some other reason this second link in the chain claiming privilege breaks. Once broken, your claim of privilege is over.

3. No lesser force will do

The easiest way to determine if lesser force will stop the threat is to ask yourself, "If I didn't have a gun, what would I do?" Then, do that. You (the armed citizen) may intentionally use only such force or threat of force that you reasonably believe is necessary to prevent or terminate the unlawful interference with your life. You may not intentionally use force which is intended or likely to cause death or great bodily harm unless you reasonably believe that such force is necessary to prevent imminent death or great bodily harm to yourself.

The level of force needed stop the threat can change during the course of an attack. The attacker may escalate the level of force by introducing a weapon or accomplices. You may need to increase the level of force needed to stop the threat.

If less than lethal force fails to stop the threat, using lethal force is justified, by definition. Lethal force begins with drawing your gun, not when you pull the trigger. Pointing a gun at an attacker has a chilling effect on their willingness to continue the attack (92 times out of 100 the attacker decides to flee). If the attacker decides to continue the attack, you must be prepared and willing to fire the gun.

This element is the third link of the chain and must be present to claim the privilege of self-defense and ceases when the threat ceases. Regardless of the level of force you used, being able to articulate your decision to use force is important.

4. Retreat is not practical

Regardless of whether Wisconsin becomes a castle doctrine state or not, retreat is a very good option if it is practical. Being practical is nothing more that weighing the level of danger in safely retreating versus the danger of staying. If you are practicing avoiding conflict and situational awareness, your intuition and instinct will warn you in advance of danger. Leaving (or retreating if practical) to avoid conflict will always be your number one best choice. The skills you learned to avoid trouble throughout your life when you were not carrying a gun become even more important to practice now that you are an armed citizen.

Retreat saves you from personal anguish, being a victim, financial distress, and allows you to maintain your constant state of peace. The wisdom of retreat is well founded.

Wisconsin does not have a statutory duty to retreat. However, the courts will instruct the jury to consider whether the opportunity to retreat was available and whether the force used was really necessary to prevent an interference with your person. This is particularly true in cases were lethal force was used. There is also an argument can be made that your decision not to retreat should call your status as a reluctant participant into question.

We consider retreat as the fourth element because of its benefits. It assists in justifying your privilege of self-defense, and more importantly, it takes you out of the position of having to defend your privilege. So as the fourth link in the chain, should the opportunity of retreat be present it should be taken.

Self-defense is a chain

Think of your right to use lethal force in self-defense as a chain that you are desperately trying to hang on to as you are dangling over a prison cell that (obviously) you do not want to fall into. The chain has exactly four links. If any *one* of those links is missing or if, at any time, any one of them breaks, your right to use or threaten lethal force ends at that very moment, and if you continue, you fall.

We have repeated "until the threat stops" a number of times because it is incredibly important. Self-defense is not about killing or even wounding an attacker. It is about stopping a threat to maintain your constant state of peace. To stay out of prison your justification to apply lethal force ends once you have stopped the threat and your use of force must end immediately.

In Wisconsin there is a second important reason. Failure to stop applying lethal force against an escaping attacker may allow the attacker to defend himself against you. This is conditional on the attacker first unsuccessfully exhausting all means of retreat. The attacker can become a reluctant participant by withdrawing from the fight in good faith and giving adequate notice thereof to you.

It is not necessary to have actually been physically harmed in order to reasonably believe that death or great bodily harm was imminent. The known threat suffices to authorize defensive action.[2]

Backwards or forwards, understanding the four elements necessary to threaten or apply lethal force is critical to saving your life and staying out of prison. Know when the four elements are present, and just as importantly, know when the chain of elements breaks.

Home Defense

The best and simplest procedure in the case of a home invasion is to retreat with your family behind you to a safe and defensible location. While the armed citizen takes the defensive position (a location, such as a hallway, where you can see the intruder moving towards you and you will have a shot) have someone else call 911 if possible. Then wait for the police to show up. If the intruder is only stealing your property, you may use any force less than lethal. You may only use lethal force if the intruder approaches your position and threatens you with death or great bodily harm. The *only* time you should even *consider* confronting the intruder is if you have to protect yourself or one of your family members.

Do not go looking for the intruder or attempt to clear your house. There are tactics for "clearing" a house, going from room to room to make sure that there are no intruders. Let the police clear your house. Clearing a house is very dangerous and police have the training, the intruder sniffing dogs, the firearms, and the body armor.

What is not required

You are not required to be psychic. It is the event that you reasonably believe to be imminent if you do nothing to stop it that matters. It is imminent in relation to time and action of the attacker not that the attacker has already attacked.

You do not have to inform the attacker of your unwillingness to be attacked or any medical condition that lower the threshold of death or great bodily harm for you.

You are not required to protect yourself. You can choose to be a victim or a survivor. It is up to you.

---

[2] Thus both the defendant and the trier of fact may consider what the defendant knew of the aggressor's violent nature, reputation for violence, customary carry of weapons, etc.

Defensive "display" and reasonable force

Defensive display of a firearm, sometimes called "brandishing," may be defined as a threat to cause death or serious bodily injury, by the production of a weapon or otherwise, so long as the actor's purpose is limited to creating an apprehension that he will use deadly force [only] if necessary. See Model Penal Code sec. 3.11(2). It does not involve the actual discharge of a firearm, for example. Nor does it constitute "use" of deadly force.

As criminal law scholar Wayne R. LaFave says:

"Merely to threaten death or serious bodily harm, without any intention to carry out the threat [unless necessary], is not to use deadly force, so that one may be justified in pointing a gun at his attacker when he would not be justified in pulling the trigger."

This is a common example of the necessity criteria in action, prohibiting greater force when lesser force will do. If the assailant continues the attack, *use* of deadly force (e.g., firing the gun) will be necessary and therefore authorized. An imminent threat is often not instantaneous. If the threat (even of death or great bodily injury) can be neutralized by a mere counter-threat, that is certainly allowable if safe for the defender, even if never mandatory. It is estimated that 98% of successful defensive gun uses involve mere brandishing. The defender demonstrates that she is capable of using deadly force, and the encounter ends as the assailant flees.

Although seldom heard of by the public except in homicide cases, justification defenses like this apply to all crimes. Thus, self-defense may be pleaded if you are charged with aggravated assault (a felony) or with assault (a misdemeanor) as a consequence of a brandishing incident.

The aftermath

Providing you are on sound legal grounds after shooting somebody, your troubles are not over. You have to deal with the aftermath of it all and it is going to be stressful. And that is the subject of the next chapter.

And remember: a gun never solves problems.

CHAPTER 5
Lethal Force and its Aftermath

If the laws about the use lethal force have not frightened you yet, or if the responsibility of carrying a gun for personal protection has not raised serious second doubts, read on.

Using lethal force in real life does not work the same way as it does on television and in the movies. Somebody who is shot is not thrown backwards several feet, or even several inches. Bullets do not go precisely where the shooter wants them under the best of circumstances. When a single bullet hits a human torso, it is unlikely to stop an attacker immediately. The impact of the bullet on the body carries no more energy than the recoil of the weapon. Remember that as the bullet travels it loses energy. The only factors you have control over is shot placement and the amount of damage done. The physics of a DGU is discussed in greater detail in the next chapter.

More importantly the justified use of lethal force may end the imminent threat, but it is only the beginning of your problems.

Again, we refer to our chapter ending warning: *a handgun does not solve problems*. By now you should understand that you are only substituting one set of problems for another. You are still alive. The question is whether you will maintain your liberty family, job and cash.

What is the best way for me to prove the facts of my DGU? How do I bring the unbiased witness forward at any place and at any time?

Proving what the attacker said after he has left the scene is incredibly difficult.

How do you refute a witness who saw only part of the attack and their story hurts your case?

We recommend using technology. Any equipment that will record audio, video or both will provide an accurate replay of the attack. At a minimum, the use of a small lightweight digital voice recorder will provide an audio record of the events. The recorder should be recording all the while you are armed in public. We know that having an accurate record has saved the liberty of the victim. Any digital recording file of an attack needs to be locked down (by you) and never erased. Purchase a recorder with a file locking feature. You can make copies, just always keep the master under your control. Also consider accessorizing with a remote microphone. Wisconsin is a "one party state" meaning that as long as one party agrees to be recorded it is legal.

You can expect the aftermath of a privileged self-defense shooting to be risky. You have survived the physical attack. You are now entering, what will become a master's program in the American Judicial System. Most people have never been arrested, never incarcerated, photographed and fingerprinted, in short have never been treated like a criminal. You may get to experience all of this and more.

Along with selecting a firearm to carry you need to find a good criminal defense attorney who has experience in Wisconsin's firearms and self-defense laws. Keep their name and number at hand and be absolutely sure the person who loves you the most knows how to contact them.

It is vital that you understand all of the above before you even think about carrying a handgun in public.

The description that follows reflects the progression of events from the moment the gun goes bang until you are free to go home. Hopefully your experience will go well should you ever have a DGU. It is impossible to cover every possible attack or outcome. We just want you prepared to deal with what typically happens.

Threat of force — is it enough?

You are armed and find yourself the victim of an attack. The vast majority of the time, when you draw or display a gun that action will end the immediate threat without a shot being fired. Your attacker will most likely flee.

Let's talk about what you say as well as what you do.

Talking yourself into trouble

From the moment you begin to act in self-defense you have to protect yourself not only from the immediate physical consequences of being the victim of a violent crime, but from the legal system as well. Everything you say and do is of vital importance. From that moment, you are no longer a citizen: You are a suspect and it is up to you to protect your rights.

Attempting to stop an attacker by saying something out of the movies is a good way to "talk" yourself into trouble. Clint Eastwood's Dirty Harry character can say, "Go ahead: make my day," when attempting to persuade somebody not to attack him. You are not Clint Eastwood.

For the armed citizen the general rule is to communicate your need for help in a way that will establish you as a victim and invite witnesses to become attentive to your situation. You want everything you say to be accurately heard and repeated by your witnesses who may only see you, hear you, or both.

Your actions will tell a story that you want witnesses to confirm. Attempting to step away from the attacker is passive behavior, not aggressive. Bad guys run from the scene, you are staying and managing the crime scene.

Actions and what you say taken in their totality will show you as the victim of an attack. Unfortunately people have been programmed to understand guns are bad. Bad guys have guns and since you have a gun, you are a bad guy. Yet you are not acting like a bad guy. Witnesses will be confused. By your actions and what you say, you are creating a picture for your witnesses that they can describe and describe accurately. Your liberty may depend on it.

Commands should be kept short, and repeated, loudly. "Stop don't hurt me; Stop don't hurt me; Stay back, stay back," are commands that instruct your attacker to leave you alone, establish you as a victim, and trigger the

Good Samaritan instincts in any witnesses to help. Ideally, anything you say when confronted with an attacker is something you would *want* to be repeated later, even if it is overheard by somebody around the corner or next door.

Yelling any form of a threat that refers to death, gun, weapon, or any type of threatening phrase will trigger the witnesses "fight or flight" syndrome. They will chose flight because they believe you are putting them in danger. Witnesses will report to the police hearing you yell threatening statements and that you threatened them.

Instead of being witnesses that can help you, their reports will assist the prosecution in sending you to prison.

Chasing an attacker

An attacker's decision to flee the scene ends the immediate threat to you and also ends your right to use force and to claim privilege of self-defense.

While the temptation to chase somebody might be understandable, do not do it. If you give chase, you are no longer a "reluctant participant," and your use of lethal force will be treated as an attack, not a defense. In Wisconsin giving chase breaks the "reluctant participant" link for you and may establish the attacker as a reluctant participant As we have mentioned, should the attacker exhaust of all means of escape he is allowed to use up to lethal force, if necessary, to stop the threat you represent to him. You have given up your privilege of self-defense.

Besides, remember the witnesses. Do you want them seeing you chasing your attacker? What if a police car pulls up just as your attacker rounds the corner, running away from you, and you have a drawn handgun?

It is not unusual for an attacker to call the police on a victim. If you have given chase you have made the attackers case that you are a threat to him.

It will not be good for you. So do not chase him.

When the attacker flees

With the four elements all present, you have displayed your firearm to an attacker to stop the threat. He decides to flee, so let him. This is the best outcome, it is the easiest situation to handle, and the one that is least likely to cause you legal trouble.

You can encourage him to leave by making it as easy as possible. Leave an escape route open if possible. *Do not* place yourself between him and the nearest exit. If you happen to find yourself blocking his exit, move aside and let him go. Make it easy on yourself, you owe it to your family.

A bonus to him fleeing is knowing that at the next meeting of the robbers and assaulters local, he will tell his buddies that there are citizens out there with guns!

Your DGU is not over. You have threatened deadly force by pointing a gun at another human being. The attacker or any witnesses may tell a very different story to the 911 operator. You do not want their version of the "truth" being the only version of the attack the police have.

You could be tempted to just walk away, but that is risky. You may have drawn the attention of somebody from a nearby house or passing car, and the only thing that they saw was you pointing a gun at your attacker. Who threatened who from the witness's point of view? When they called 911, what do you think they will report?

Remember following your decision to take action, you will have to defend yourself from the legal system. This begins with your 911 call and what you say. You need to protect your rights so only provide enough information to establish yourself as the victim. Immediately call 911 and report, for example: "I've had a defensive gun use at Ninth and Elm. I defended myself and the attacker has run away. The attacker was a tall, thin white man with black hair, a blue jean jacket and tan pants. He ran down Elm to the south. No one was hurt and I'm safe now. My name is John Jones. I will file a complaint once I have been able to consult with my attorney." Then immediately get off the phone and call your attorney. Pointing a gun at someone is a crime and you are in trouble, at least temporarily. You need an attorney to assist you in establishing your claim of privilege of self-defense. Even the short 911 call tells law enforcement that there is another story to sort out. Remember the attacker may have already made a 911 call implicating you as the bad guy.

During your 911 call you may be instructed to wait there for the police. When the police arrive, they should find you with your ID and license in hand, and your gun holstered. Your story should be very short, and entirely factual. Any deeper discussion should be avoided for the time being. You can say, "A man attacked me; here's his description. I defended myself and he ran away, I'm very scared and upset, and (finally) I need to talk to my attorney. I do not consent to any search or any seizure."

Why? They'll ask. "You were the victim, right? All you have to do is talk to us. Let's just clear this up right away."

Do not start gabbing. You are in no condition to protect yourself from confusion in the investigation. You are not your best representative at this time. "I need to talk to my attorney," is *all* you need to say at that point, although you may have to repeat it. And then, you say nothing at all, until you have talked to your attorney.

You are going through an extremely stressful experience and the police know it. Your brain wants to make sense out of the nonsense of what just happened. Again, rational thought is going to be very difficult because your brain has blocked out any information it did not feel necessary to your survival. Talking now is risky because when you are not thinking clearly you may inadvertently use words that hurt your position rather than help it. For example, there is a great difference of meaning between saying "so I shot him," and "so I shot to stop the threat." Expect your words to be recorded and become part of the evidence against you. Admitting on tape that you "shot him" does you no good. Police have no duty to find evidence to exonerate you.

When the attacker surrenders

There are two important considerations regarding an attacker surrendering.

First, do you know if the surrender is a ruse which is a part of the attack? It is almost impossible to determine if the first attacker has you doing things that you are totally unprepared to do, such as holding your attacker for police. Since you do not have eyes in the back of your head, get to a place where you are minimally exposed to a continued attack from a direction that is difficult to cover. The safest place to be is at the attacker's feet with him face down on the ground.

You are in a very dangerous situation and you may not assume the scene is safe. Now you must observe both the surrendering attacker and the rest of the scene for possible accomplices. Should the attacker decide to flee at this point let him go and call 911 to report the attack as described above. Remember that blocking his escape can lead to the attacker becoming a reluctant participant and then be allowed to use force, including lethal force, against you.

The second consideration is the laws of Wisconsin regarding unlawful detention of another. There are a number of crimes with which you may be charged including, false imprisonment, which is a felony (Wis. Stat. 940.30), endangering safety by use of dangerous weapon, class A misdemeanor, (Wis. Stat. 941.20), recklessly endangering safety, a felony (Wis. Stat. 941.30). What this really means is, do not hold an attacker if at all possible. The physical and legal consequences are just too high.

The district attorneys have a great deal of prosecutorial discretion. How perfect your actions were may keep you out of prison, but do not count on it. You may also be charged with these crimes should your claimed privilege of self-defense fail.

When the attack continues

The last, and most dangerous (and, thankfully, very unlikely) possibility is that you will actually need to use deadly force: shoot an attacker in order to prevent him from killing or seriously hurting you.

The physics of a lethal confrontation

Newton's Laws apply in real life. Firing a shot sufficient to lift an attacker off his feet and knock him back several feet would have a similar effect on the shooter. In Hollywood, the effect is accomplished by a harness attached to the actor being shot and several burly grips yanking on the rope attached to it.

In real life, this simply does not happen. Newton's Laws are not repealed on the street. Even if your first shot stops the attack it will not be anything as dramatic as your attacker flying backward. He might appear to stumble or fall (almost certainly forward). It is possible that your first shot will physically incapacitate him immediately and it is certainly possible that it will change his mind.

Or, quite possibly, he will simply continue with his attack.

The physiology of a lethal confrontation

Adrenaline has both physical and psychological effects, and the threat of a violent confrontation is certain to cause your adrenal gland to produce and deliver a massive amount adrenaline into your system with a huge complex of effects you the victim. The attacker, when presented with an armed citizen is likely to also have a large dose of adrenaline introduced into his system.

Your adrenaline charged body is now ready for battle. Several physiological effects will come into play.

Vision tends to narrow

This is the so-called "tunnel vision" effect where it becomes difficult or impossible to see anything besides the threat. This is also called "target fixation." In more than one instance this fixation has caused the victim to shoot the attacker's gun. Train yourself not to look at the weapon but at the center of mass at whatever part the attacker presents and shoot there. Shooting center of mass will lower the likelihood of a miss.

Strength goes up

This is why light triggers on self-defense weapons are such a bad idea. What feels like simply resting a finger on the trigger may result in unintentionally firing it. If you have a light trigger pull, it is extremely important that you *must* keep your finger off the trigger until you are ready to shoot.

Dexterity drops

Your dexterity drops as does the ability to perform complex tasks. This is why external safeties are dangerous. Heck, you may not even remember you have one and that it is engaged. Easy-to-operate, uncomplicated handguns are better for self-defense.

The perception of time changes

This is known as the tachypsychia (literally, *the speed of mind*) effect. Things may seem to happen in slow motion, or to speed up. This is one of the many reasons not to be too quick to talk to police afterwards. You might honestly say that a confrontation took two or three minutes when it really only took a few seconds. Police officers and prosecutors are not always very sensitive to the difference between an honest misstatement and a misrepresentation. A digital voice recorder will give the actual duration of the attack.

Auditory exclusion

Most hunters will report ignoring the loud report of a rifle when they have shot a deer. The same is likely to be true during a violent confrontation. However, that same report will often be uncomfortable even with hearing protection on the range. The sound of your firearm is the same. Your mind is processing that information differently.

The ability to feel pain drops.

Pain is irrelevant to survival and is commonly suppressed until sometime later. In order to be a factor, pain first must be perceived, and second, it must cause an emotional response. Ronald Reagan did not even know he was shot by Hinkley until he was in the car and being examined by a secret service agent.

Psychological splitting

You may have an "out-of-body" sensation. You can still direct your body and its functions, but you are watching events as an outside observer.

Physiologically, when under attack, your body will engage your "fight or flight" survival patterns. Your will resort to your most basic survival skills and your training.

Remember Maslow's Hierarchy of Human Needs, that after our need to maintain life (breathing, eating, and maintaining body temperature) is our need to be safe.

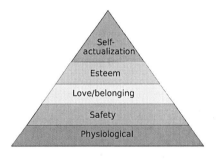

Your response to an attack will be as automatic a response as you may ever experience. Your training of what to do to survive an attack will take over. So, the more you train, the better your response to an attack will be.

Rational thought becomes difficult

According to Artwohl and Christensen[3], your cognition also changes when you are under attack and in what they call a "high-arousal state":

> "Experiential thinking is the kind of thinking that will automatically kick in whenever you perceive a threat and your body is flooded with natural drugs that induce the high arousal state. Under threat conditions, experiential thinking will dominate and reduce or even eliminate your ability to think

---

[3] Dr. Alexis Artwohl, Loren W. Christensen, *Deadly Force Encounters: What Cops Need to Know to Mentally and Physically Prepare for and Survive a Gunfight* at 45-46 (Paladin Press, 1997).

in a rational, creative, and reflective manner. It is effortless, automatic, lightning quick, action-oriented, and much more efficient (but not necessarily more accurate) than rational thinking. It is experienced as much more compelling than rational thinking...

Experiential thinking is also what you do when you follow your gut instinct. There is nothing mystical about gut instincts, sixth sense, or intuition. Our brain is an incredible computer constantly analyzing subtle bits of information to reach conclusions, information that may not be obvious to our conscious awareness. You know your conclusion is right, but you can't explain exactly how you know that (of course, your conclusion could also be wrong).

Experiential thinking does not follow a step-by-step process to reach a conclusion but reaches it quickly without your knowing how it got there. You must rely on this type of thinking when you do not have enough time or information to reach a carefully reasoned, logical conclusion."

Having the "four elements" so well engrained into your psyche as to influence your experiential thinking will allow you to recognize when the four links of the chain are present very quickly. You must rely on this type of thinking to keep you out of prison, therefore, the better equip your mind is the more likely you will be successful.

All of these effects apply to both the victim of the attack and the attacker, and must be taken into account. The sort of pain that would normally stop somebody in their tracks may well have no immediate effect on a determined attacker. This is why defensive measures like pepper spray are much more effective on volunteer test subjects than real-life attackers.

It is entirely possible for either the attacker or the victim, or both, to continue fighting even after being seriously, and perhaps even fatally, wounded. Shear emotion such as rage or hate can keep a grievously injured person fighting. One video, available on the Internet, shows a bank robber struggling with a guard for several long seconds after being shot in the heart, only to flee and drop dead in the parking lot outside the bank—and, again, he had been shot in the *heart*. Humans, like deer, will have enough oxygen remaining in the brain for full voluntary function for ten to fifteen seconds after being shot in the heart. Only a shot that disrupts the brain or upper spinal cord will cause an immediate end to an attack.

This is why the legal principle that lethal force is justified until the threat ends is so important.

If the attacker continues the attack, even if the wounds he has already received will later prove fatal, until the threat ceases it is not only lawful to continue shooting, it is necessary.

The right to use lethal force ends when the attacker stops attacking, but *the event* does not end until the attacker no longer represents a threat of death or great bodily harm. If it becomes necessary to shoot an attacker, it is justified to continue shooting until the attack stops, or any one link of the chain of the four elements breaks.

It may take one shot for that to happen, or it may take many shots.

You may not even see the shots landing. On a well-lighted pistol range, a sharp hole against a target will be easily visible at close range, but violent confrontations rarely take place in well-lighted areas. Even in good light, a wound may be hidden by the pattern of the attacker's clothing, even if it immediately starts bleeding.

The physical effects of a shooting

There is no way to discuss the effects of a shooting without discussing some awful facts.

The most important one is that shooting somebody in order to physically stop an attack requires doing a lot of damage to another human being, damage that is entirely likely to be fatal. We wish this were not so: (electronic weapons are also permitted under Wisconsin's license to carry act. We will discuss these in the chapter on selecting a weapon).

Handguns are damaging but not necessarily incapacitating. If the first shot stops the attacker it is more likely because he has changed his mind, not because he is unable to continue. This is a very good outcome.

A single shot can be reliably counted on to immediately incapacitate an attacker if it severs the upper spinal cord. If that happens the nerves will be unable to carry information below the cut or break and the attack will stop. The attacker will simply collapse as his brain will no longer be able to send information to his muscles.

The second way to immediately incapacitate an attacker is a shot to the brain which is also very difficult. Sufficient damage to an attacker's brain will end his ability to continue the attack. But the skull is thick, and the head is a small target under the best of circumstances, much less during a frightening confrontation where the person being attacked will literally be unable to concentrate on his handgun's sights, focusing instead on the attacker. Also, the head may be moving from side to side. There are a lot of important body parts in the chest, the heart and lungs, for example. Shots to the torso, may incapacitate the attacker, but this will take more time.

And if the bullet misses, it will go on until it hits something. The odds of you being attacked in front of a tall earthen berm where you do not have to worry about a bullet doing anything other than burying it in the ground are very small.

This is why almost all self-defense instructors teach that defensive shots should be aimed or pointed at the attacker's center of mass or whatever is presented as the target and that you should continue to fire until the threat ends.

Some instructors train students to do a "double-tap" firing twice, and then re-evaluating. Other instructors suggest that three shots, two to the chest and one to the pelvis, and then a very quick assessment of the threat is a better course of action. Never take your eyes off the threat until you are sure it has ceased to be a threat. Do not re-holster your firearm and then find out that you are still under attack.

After the confrontation it is important for your attorney to be able to assert that you fired only as long as it was legally permissible and then immediately stopped. One shot may stop the attack while three may be insufficient. "Why did your client shoot his attacker four times?" the prosecutor might ask your attorney. "Because the first three shots didn't stop the attack," will be the answer. "The fourth did that is why he didn't shoot five or six times."[4]

Firing toward center of mass also has other advantages. With a handgun that fits you correctly it is easy, after very little training, to make tight shot groups in targets at five to ten feet which are self-defense distances. When under attack and with your adrenaline pumping and eyes fixed on the attacker, it is unlikely your sights will be useful. Shooting under these stressful conditions is difficult. This is another reason training and practice is so important.

---

[4] The authors are aware of defensive shootings in which 13 or even 33 hits did not end the threat. The next hit did and it was, properly, the last shot fired.

A center of mass shot permits you to hit the attacker at a maximum possible distance and not have the bullet miss the attacker. It is hard to think about this while in fear of your life, but you do have to consider where your bullets might go if you miss. A missed shot can travel a long way, and can easily hurt or kill an innocent person.

This leads to the key point: when a life-threatening confrontation is unavoidable, it is necessary to first survive it physically, and then be prepared to survive the attack morally, legally and financially.

Remember physical consequences of a justified self-defense shooting are just the beginning of the victim's problems. While still recovering from the trauma of the experience, it will be necessary to deal with the police, the legal system, and the court of public opinion just as it will be if the attacker flees or surrenders.

It is going to be long and uncomfortable, and there is just no way around it.

After a lethal confrontation

The immediate problem of being killed by the attacker ends when he either flees, surrenders, or is no longer able to attack because he has been sufficiently damaged. But other problems are just beginning.

As soon as you take out a firearm in a DGU, much less actually pull the trigger, you have become a suspect, and are going to remain one at least until the investigation is concluded. Unless your claim of privilege stands, you may be a defendant in a criminal case and in a civil lawsuit.

Your immediate concern should be to call the police and an ambulance if necessary. Even if you have injured or killed somebody in self-defense, there is a legal obligation to see that aid is rendered. You failure to do so may become a chargeable offense even if your claim of privilege was justified.

The next concern should be to avoid being shot by the police when they arrive on the scene. If at all possible ask the 911 operator to describe you to the responding officers and tell them you are not a threat to them and you will cooperate with all of their commands.

To claim privilege of self-defense you must be willing to act like a sheepdog. A wolf will run from his crime scene, witnesses will remain and be confused. You must remain. You have a right to find a way to be safe, but are a part of the crime scene. So *do not* run away, except if necessary for safety. This is true when the attacker flees, and it is just as true if you had to shoot him. Running from the scene of a shooting may be taken by police, prosecutors, and courts as a sign of guilt and should be avoided. Altering the crime scene or concealing evidence is also a big No-No.

Modern forensic science is increasingly good, and gun shop advice to "if he drops outside your front door, just drag him back in" should be politely ignored. You can and should protect all the evidence you can. You cannot and should not alter, change, move, discard, destroy, lose or in any other way mess with evidence. It is not only illegal and immoral, it is bad strategy. *Leave the evidence alone.*

Now call 911, or have somebody else do so. Having another person make the 911 call will identify at least one witness who may be helpful to you.

As discussed earlier, the conversation should be kept *short* and factual. "I have had a defensive gun use at (the address or location) and need the police and an ambulance." After that, it is best just to get off the line. There is no need to have your excited adrenaline driven babbling report of the details of the shooting preserved as evidence on the 911 recording. Your do not talk alarm should be loudly ringing. "Anything you say can and will be used against you in a court of law" no matter who you have said anything to.

This requires a firm intention—the 911 operator will instruct you to stay on the line and keep talking. That is what they are trained to do, which is understandable. The more information police and emergency services have, the better they can do their jobs, and an important part of the job of the police is to collect and preserve evidence for your prosecution.

When the police arrive

There are several principles involved in being prepared for the arrival of the police.

The most important one is this: *after using or threatening deadly force, the police are not your friends.*

That is worth repeating. *After using or threatening deadly force, the police are not your friends.*

They will not see themselves as your friends either. It may suit an investigator to portray himself as sympathetic to you in order to draw out information and to get you to talk about what happened. They will be coming into the situation cold, knowing nothing more than that they have been summoned to the scene of an attack. Police routinely see the aftermath of many shootings and few of them are done in self-defense.

At a crime scene police are trained to do certain things and considering you as a victim is not one of them. As the adage says, "when hearing hoof beats, think horses not zebras."

When police are summoned to a shooting, they think about a man with gun, assault and attempted murder, not a justifiable defensive gun use. Same for when they hear about somebody pointing a gun at somebody. It is understandable. From a police officer's point of view, an armed criminal, assault, robbery, attempted murder, and murder are the "horses," and defensive gun uses are the "zebras." You are a victim, a zebra.

It is important to be as non-threatening to the police as possible when they arrive on the scene. If it is safe to do so, if the attacker is unable to resume the attack, or has fled, the gun should be holstered. If not, it is important to remember to keep it pointed in a safe direction, with your finger off the trigger. If possible, somebody else should be sent to meet the police when they arrive, to tell them there is no present danger, to describe the victim, "She's a small, black woman wearing a white coat, and she's the victim." The attacker is lying on the floor." Repeat that there is no present danger.

Remember your hands. Police officers love to see hands. At this point, your hands should be *visible* and *empty*, if at all possible.

Most of what you should do is just common sense. Follow police directions as to what to do. Cooperate immediately,[5] communicate what you are doing, and make no sudden movements that can be misinterpreted.

When it comes to action, as opposed to discussion, compliance is mandatory. Be as calm as you can be polite and cooperative. After all, you have called the police to come to preserve evidence you will need in your defense.

---

[5] This is one of the reasons that your defensive handgun must be reliable, both in terms of it firing when you pull the trigger, and of not firing when you don't. The police officer should tell you to "put the weapon down", but if he or she says, "Drop the gun!" do it without it making a loud bang. If the responding officers give you inconsistent commands, such as one shouts "Don't move" while another is screaming "Get outta the car," your best tactic is to freeze. They'll take you down physically, probably with some bruises, but you won't get shot for moving. The authors know of several cases where civilians died while trying to comply with confusing commands. If in doubt, freeze.

It is necessary to protect yourself from the legal system, and that largely consists of two things: saying as little as possible and immediately consulting with a good attorney who is experienced in criminal matters.

As an aside, how you are treated by the police is very likely to be directly proportional to the age and experience of the first officers on the scene. Older and more experienced officers will be able to assess your situation using their years of experience. They also have refined interrogative experience. That said, as the scene is assessed, senior officers (especially beat officers) will figure out what happened fairly quickly. If a "wet behind the ears" rookie is running the scene, be ready for by-the-book treatment. Record names and badge numbers if necessary and deal with any mistreatment later.

Establishing victimhood

What you say to the police when they arrive is critical. As said before, police are trained to see you as a suspect. You need to get them to report you as the victim. Most important is that you do not say too much. They are going to need some very basic information and this is your opportunity to point out evidence they may overlook. Once you have worked through the four statements it is time shut up. It is time to exercise your right to remain silent. It is not the job of the police to determine your guilt or innocents, it is their job to collect and preserve evidence. A guide to help you communicate with police and yet not say too much was developed by Massad Ayoob.

> Massad F. Ayoob is an internationally known firearms and self-defense instructor. He has taught police techniques and civilian self-defense to both law enforcement officers and private citizens in numerous venues since 1974. He was the director of the Lethal Force Institute (LFI) from 1981 to 2009, and he now directs the Massad Ayoob Group (MAG). Ayoob has appeared as an expert witness in number of trials.
>
> Ayoob has authored several books and more than 1,000 articles on firearms, combat techniques, self-defense, and legal issues, and has served in an editorial capacity for *Guns Magazine*, *American Handgunner*, *Gun Week*, and *Combat Handguns*.

Massad recommends making the following four statements: "He attacked me," followed by "I will sign a complaint," "there is the evidence," and "I need to talk to my lawyer before I say anything else." As a matter of law, a demand to consult with an attorney cannot be used as evidence of guilt. Also state that you do not consent to any search or seizure. Do not expect that the police will treat you that way.

By limiting your comments to police, using Massad's four statements you may improve your case. Your goal is to have the police report to reflect you as the victim (not a wolf), include evidence to support your position as the victim and your willingness in prosecuting the attacker while preserving your rights.

"He attacked me"

It is not a problem to say that you were attacked. It does not, in and of itself, admit the use of deadly force, but it is an important part of the privilege for it. Privilege is what is called in law an "affirmative defense." When claiming "he attacked me" you are inferring that you have absolute standing as a reluctant participant. You did nothing to provoke, precipitate or participate in the altercation.

Going beyond "he attacked me" to "so I shot him" is an admission that, if you need to make it, you can make it later on the advice of an attorney.

It is best not to start talking. You might not be able to stop and will likely do yourself more harm. Understand that the possibility of arrest is about the same as the sun coming up tomorrow. If you cannot limit your comments to Massad's "He attacked me" then *Do not talk.*

There is no advantage, and much disadvantage, to discussing any of the details of the incident then and there. Anything you say about the exact details of the attack can and will be examined for possible vulnerabilities and compared with later statements, and can easily be used to suggest that you have changed your story rather than that you have said the same thing in different ways. If you tell what happened then but leave out an important element, it is likely that you will be accused of "conveniently" remembering it later or that you are lying. Here the digital voice recorder will allow you accurately recall and retell the attack. You should not make a statement right then and there. It needs to be done later with your attorney's assistance.

And there are questions you cannot answer without the answers being used against you, like "Were you angry at him?" If you say yes, then it can be argued that you shot him because you were angry at him. If you say no, then you are a liar—how could anybody not be angry at somebody who tried to kill him.

The simple way to avoid any possibility of either misinterpretation or being accused of lying is to say as little as possible.

What you *do not* say *cannot* be used against you, thanks to your Fifth Amendment right against self-incrimination.

"He attacked me" is all you need to say on that subject before talking to your lawyer. That will get the police on the right track.

"I will sign a complaint"

This does not mean right now. Writing out and signing a complaint needs the advice of your attorney. If the police officer responds by saying, "Fine, just write down what happened," the only safe response is, "I'll be happy to, just as soon as I've talked with my attorney," and repeat that as many times as necessary.

Saying "I will sign a complaint" *is not* a commitment to talk further. What it does is imbed in the police report that you were the victim. It indicates to the prosecuting attorney that you are willing to help them put your attacker behind bars.

Police understand that the perpetrator signs a confession, and the *victim* signs a complaint. By saying, "I will sign a complaint," you are saying to them, in language they understand, that you are the victim. If they do not want to arrest you, this helps to give them justification for it.

Realistically, the police *will* arrest you most of the time. The only thing they know for sure is that there has been a shooting, and they have every reason to believe that the victim has shot somebody. Whether or not it was a privileged shooting is a decision they must leave to others.

"There is the evidence"

Police officers are humans, and humans can make mistakes. They can suffer from perception warps. Shell casings from the attacker's handgun can be stepped on; a knife can be overlooked; or a baseball bat, tire iron, or claw hammer might not even be seen as a weapon and not taken into evidence even though the attacker's fingerprints on it can be very important. The police were not present at your attack. It is vital from your point of view that none of the evidence be overlooked or damaged. Gathering evidence is what the police do.

Evidence is not just physical evidence. It is perfectly reasonable to point to witnesses, or to suggest that somebody in a nearby building might have overheard the confrontation. Look for cameras on buildings, in parking lots, or people with cell phones.

The behavior of the attacker may also be important evidence. Was his behavior erratic and possibly drug induced? Had he been drinking? Are there prescription drugs on his person?

What you want to project, without going into detail, is that you were defending yourself and expect the evidence to support your claim.

But that does not mean keep talking. You need to immediately go to the next step:

"I need to talk to my lawyer,
I do not consent to any search,
I do not consent to any seizure"

This is the most important part of the formula, and you are likely to need to repeat it. As you can see, this is a slight variation on Ayoob's four-point strategy: explicitly saying that you do not consent to any search or seizure.

This fourth step is the part that *cannot be skipped*. Those who are concerned that if they start talking they might have trouble stopping, should just skip right to this step. "*I need to talk to my lawyer and I do not consent to any search or seizure.*"

This is your security blanket: "*I need to talk to my lawyer, and I do not consent to any search or seizure.*" Keep repeating it until the police allow you to speak with your lawyer. Never, *ever*, consent to any search or seizure. Experienced criminal law specialists advise that there is no upside to consenting.

Why not talk?

Ayoob, who trains police officers who investigate police-involved shootings, recommends that any interview with the officer take place at a later time. An officer who has been involved in a shooting may say something, innocuous in context, or a heated exclamation showing how angry the officer is that can be used to suggest that he acted improperly.

Ayoob is not alone in this.

IACP, the International Association of Chiefs of Police, strongly recommends that police officers *not* be interviewed immediately after a shooting:

> *...the officer can benefit from some recovery time before detailed interviewing begins. This can range from a few hours to overnight, depending on the emotional state of the officer and the circumstances. Officers who have been afforded this opportunity to calm down are likely to provide a more coherent and accurate statement. [emphasis added]*

Realistically, there is nothing you (an armed citizen) can do to avoid the likelihood of being arrested after a shooting, and what you need to focus on is minimizing the damage anything you said might cause. The best strategy is to consider yourself under arrest form the moment you pull the trigger. Think "anything you say (or do) can be used against you in a court of law".

One common investigative technique is for an officer to portray himself as one who is sympathetic to the suspect who only needs a few questions cleared up before closing the whole matter. It is a simple play to the victim's need for security and certainty in a stressful, strange, and uncertain situation. By considering yourself under arrest, you can better control the outcome. In the wake of a shooting, talking to a policeman before consulting with an attorney is a risky proposition of dubious possible benefit.

So do not do it. Just repeat *"I want my lawyer, and I do not consent to any search or seizure."*

What the police will do

While physical abuse and some forms of intimidation are illegal and rare (but not unknown) there are forms of intimidation and influence that courts have not only said are completely legal, but which are part of police officers' training.

David Kopel, a leading civil rights attorney specializing in advocacy for self-defense issues, points to the research of Richard A. Leo, Ph.D., J.D., Associate Professor of Criminology, Law and Society, and an Associate Professor of Psychology and Social Behavior at the University of California, Irvine.

Leo's research shows that police routinely use "techniques of neutralization" in an attempt to get you to talk and to keep you talking.

These can involve telling you that the interrogator thinks you have not done anything wrong, that the attacker deserved what happened: that you have committed a crime, but only a minor one, say, that your attacker was just slightly injured and is, even at this moment, being booked, and that all the investigator needs is for you to write out and sign a complaint.

Any or all of that could be true.

Any or all of that could be false.

You do not know.

You should not talk.

The investigator could think that you have committed murder and wants to get more evidence. He may believe that the person you shot deserved it in a moral sense, but you are still guilty of a crime for having shot him. And it is entirely possible that the hypothetical attacker, instead of now being booked, is lying dead in the morgue and the police are gathering evidence that will be used to prosecute you and would love for you to help them with that.

There is no way to know, and until your lawyer tells you otherwise, you simply should not say anything except, "I want to speak to my attorney, and I do not consent to any search or seizure." If you find that you have to keep repeating that, fine.

The relationship between police and suspects is disproportionate in favor of the police. While citizens are not permitted to lie to the police, the police, in fact, *are permitted to lie* to suspects and frequently do. They can, with utter impunity, say that if you talk to them you will not be arrested, and then arrest you after you talk.

The police may explain that it is in your best interest to get your side of the story on the record without getting lawyers involved ("It'll look bad if you do not talk now, Bob") and that letting you explain what happened is something they are doing as a favor to you, even though they know it is not.

If they have two suspects they can put both of them in the back of a police car and leave them alone to talk to each other with the hidden video camera in the front of the car taping the conversation. Or, separate the suspects and pit one against the other.

These are a couple of examples of investigative techniques an investigator can use. It is the job of police investigators is to get as much information as possible to support a charge and conviction for the prosecutor to sort out.

And there is another dynamic to the investigation.

To the extent that an interrogation is a battle of wits, the opponents are not equal.

The police investigator is experienced at this. He interrogates people on a daily basis and may have been doing it for decades.

You have gone through your entire life without being the subject of a police interrogation at all. Most likely the closest you have been to one is watching one on television.

Getting involved in this is like somebody who has never picked up a tennis racket going out on the court against a professional tennis player, except, in the case of a police interrogation, there is a lot more to lose than a tennis match.

It is actually much worse than that. When you go into a tennis match you are not frightened half out of your wits. The minutes and hours after you have been forced into a defensive gun use is not a time when you can coolly and calmly answer questions or explain yourself, and it certainly is not a time when you will be thinking about all the implications of the various laws involved.

Realistically anybody involved in a defensive gun use will need the help of an experienced criminal attorney and must not talk with the police, except as above. There is no way you can avoid the necessity and cost of a good lawyer. Any attempt to "do it yourself" is just going to cost you money (if you are lucky) or years of freedom (if you botch the job). Leave your defense to the professionals!

If it turns out that a police interview is in your interest, the attorney can and should participate in the interview. Many criminal attorneys will simply refuse to have their clients take an interview at all and submit a sworn statement instead.

Finally, your attacker is unlikely to consider whether your lawyer will be immediately available when he attacks you. It is possible that your attorney will be in court, at a dinner party, playing golf or at the kid's hockey game. If you are attacked late in the evening, call the "person who loves you the most" and who will move heaven and earth to get you representation immediately. Being represented by someone familiar with the legal system and whose head is much clearer than yours is the important thing.

When are you under arrest?

If police officers have said, "I'm placing you under arrest," it is fair to assume that you are. But, even if they have not formally made that statement, you might be.

Take a hypothetical case: you are sitting in a room at a police station, behind a table, with two plainclothes detectives on the other side of the table between you and the door. A third, uniformed officer is standing in front of the door. Are you under arrest, or are you voluntarily chatting with the police and free to leave at any time?

Asking, "Am I under arrest? " is the obvious thing to do, but it will not do any good. Feel free to try it.

"Why, *should* you be under arrest? Have you done something wrong?" is the standard comeback and both an attempt to change the subject and an invitation to talk. Ask, "Am I free to leave?" If not, assume that "Anything you say can and will be used against you."

If you are under arrest you have the right to talk to your lawyer. The police must make a telephone available for you to call him or her, and cannot question you further after you have demanded to talk to your lawyer unless you choose to waive that right, something they will be only too happy to let you do. Remember, if you still have your recorder keep it running.

If you are not under arrest or not the subject of a "Terry stop" you are free to leave. However, the police do not have to do anything to help you because you are free to walk out the door. If you stay, the court will take anything you say as a voluntary consensual conversation.

Can you walk out that door?

There is only one way to make your custodial status clear: try to leave.

In that situation, if you get up and quietly but firmly say, "I'm going to leave now," and walk toward the door, perhaps saying, "Excuse me, I need for you to step aside so I can leave" to the officer standing in front of the door, one of two things will happen: either you will be allowed to leave or you will be informed that you are under arrest, in which case you still must continue to demand to speak to your attorney, and never consent to any search or seizure.

Not talking is not just for you

Not talking to the police does not just apply to you as the victim. The prosecutor may subpoena anyone with whom you have spoken. Certain family members, your spiritual leader and your attorney may avoid answering questions.

If the victim and the attacker knew each other, the police will proceed on the assumption that there was a previous history of problems between the two and attempt to find out details about it. Anything said by a family member for example regarding you and your attacker once having harsh words can be used as evidence against you. Family members should be instructed that they are not to open the door to policemen who do not have warrants, and to always explain that:

1. They will be happy to have a conversation with any investigators as soon as they have talked to their attorney, and
2. They do not consent to any search or seizure.
3. They must not talk further until their attorney tells them otherwise.
4. Do not talk with the news media, even if they offer you anonymity.
5. Stay off the internet, especially blogs regarding the incident.

This is advice your attorney should give you. If they do not tell you to sit tight and let them handle it, get a different attorney.

Most of the time a law-abiding citizen, sees the police as allies. They are the folks you call when you hear a suspicious sound in the alley outside your house at night. When you encounter a policeman working overtime at the local supermarket, you know he is there to protect the supermarket and you probably give him a smile and a nod. Even when a police officer stops you for having a turn signal out or a minor traffic violation, he is doing his job, and it is just not a big deal, so you do not treat the police officer as somebody who is endangering your freedom.

This is our relationship with police most of the time and under ordinary circumstances. But after using or threatening deadly force, everything changes. To the police officer, you are no longer an ordinary citizen. You are a suspect, and, once again:

After you use a gun in self-defense, the police are not your friends.

This may sound paranoid to some, but for anyone who has been the subject of a police investigation, paranoia like this has become good policy.

The risks of talking are huge, and offer few benefits. We do keep repeating this, and we hope we're not boring you, but this is so important that it probably can't be repeated too often; "I want my attorney"

We like Massad's four statements and you should be sure that you can follow them. They help to position you as the victim. But do remember that the fourth point; the *request* for your lawyer, the *refusal* to consent to any search or seizure, and *not talking after*—is the most important part of it.

After a nonlethal confrontation

The same principles apply to the majority of defensive gun uses in which no shot is fired. If anything, these situations can be more complicated. While in the case of a successful defensive shooting, the attacker is either dead or seriously injured and unlikely to be able to immediately or ever spin the situation to his advantage, if the attacker has simply fled or is still on the scene, uninjured, when the police arrive—he will not be at that disadvantage.

Another actual case from another state (the names have been changed) is worth looking at.

Bob carried a handgun daily to protect the large sums of cash that his business requires that he carry about with him.

One day, he was involved in a small traffic accident in which the driver of another car backed into him, causing no serious damage to his car, but jamming him up against the curb. The other driver came out of the car with a tire iron, saying, "I'm going to beat your head in," and added some colorful expletives as he moved toward Bob.

Believing, reasonably, that he was in immediate danger of having his head beaten in, and retreat not being practical, Bob drew his handgun and pointed it at the attacker at which point the attacker broke off the attack, retreated to his own car, and drove off.

Bob, thinking that the incident was over, simply drove home. There was, shortly, a knock on his door, and two uniformed police officers asked if they could come in to talk to him, which he agreed to. They asked him some details about the incident, which he answered thoroughly and honestly, if somewhat heatedly, at which point they asked if he could produce the gun that he had been carrying and the carry license under which it was legal for him to carry it.

He produced both; the policemen seized both, and promptly arrested him on felony charges, at which time he finally contacted an experienced criminal attorney. After some negotiation with the prosecutor's office, his attorney managed to get the charges reduced to a misdemeanor, provided he pled guilty, surrendered his carry license, and made no attempt to have his handgun returned to him.

Bob made several mistakes and was fortunate enough to have gotten off so easily.

His first mistake was not immediately calling the police to report the DGU. It is an understandable reluctance but a critical error. Bob had a defensive gun use and had drawn a gun and pointed it at somebody. But his reluctance to call the police allowed the attacker time to get the first report into the police thereby framing the "facts" of the altercation. It is called "the race to the courthouse," and he let his attacker win by default.

His second mistake was not calling his lawyer.

His third mistake was to let the police into his home and talk with them. This was a particularly bad idea. An interview with the police should be on Bob's terms and conducted with his attorney present.

Bob had no obligation to open the door to the police or to answer their questions. Producing his handgun and license was misrepresented as required. Bob should have required the police to produce a search warrant and made contact with his attorney before answering officer's questions. He got suckered into an interview that had significant risk and little chance of reward.

When the four elements are present and you decide to produce a firearm, even if you do not pull the trigger, the most important things to do are:

1. *call* the police (you or preferably a witness if any)
2. *call* your lawyer
3. *refuse* to consent to any search or seizure
4. *remember* Massad Ayoob's four statements
5. *say nothing* more until after talking with your attorney.

If you remember nothing else from this book, remember that.

Getting sued

As if being almost certainly arrested and quite possibly charged with a crime is not bad enough if you have a defensive gun use, there is also the risk of being sued.

Currently (7/2011) you can be civilly sued even if found innocent of criminal charges. The most effective response to a civil suit is having the proper liability insurance. We cannot recommend or suggest any agent or any insurance company but there are good insurance companies that will insure you for using reasonable force to protect yourself. It is better to know that you have coverage before the gun goes bang, then to be told there is no coverage after the gun goes bang.

Financing a Defensive Gun Use

Armed citizens know that the need to shoot someone is a low probability and high consequence event. Although you may never have needed to use a gun in self defense, we know that low probability is not the same thing as zero probability. Threats to your personal safety are increasing daily, which increase the odds that in the future you may need to use your gun someday to protect your life. Unfortunately, America is becoming a more dangerous place to live every day.

So, are you going to bet everything you own and maybe your future earnings that you will never need to use your gun? Have you considered how you will pay for an attorney and possible damages should you ever have to use a gun to save your life? Most armed citizens find out at the worst possible time that they could not afford to use their gun. Just ask George Zimmerman. After three years, and over $3,000,000 spent on attorneys, the Government finally gave up looking for a way to prosecute him for a righteous shooting. This is in addition to the cost of his defense during the criminal trial. Zimmerman is millions of dollars in debt now. Saving his life financially ruined Zimmerman, but you don't have to be ruined financially with a little advanced planning.

I am not selling insurance nor am I paid any money to tell you about this. I want you to know where to look for coverage in your current Homeowner's policy if it is there, or what questions you will need to ask your current insurance agent if it isn't. It may turn out that you will have to change your insurer your agent or both, for you to become properly insured. This coverage is either in your policy or it isn't. Your Homeowner's policy cannot be endorsed to add back this coverage, which is why your changing insurer and/or agent may be necessary.

Several organizations do sell stand alone "self defense" or "gun use" "policies". Some of these are nothing more than pre-paid legal plans or very limited liability policies. Before you buy one of these, obtain a specimen policy and ask your insurance agent to review it for you. Unlike your Auto insurance or Homeowner's policies which are "pay on your behalf" policies, many of these "self defense" or "gun use" type policies are an "indemnification" policy. What is the big difference you may be thinking? Well, a "pay on behalf" policy literally stands in your shoes and pays all your defense costs for you. An "indemnification" policy will expect you to pay for everything yourself first, and then they may "indemnify" or reimburse you for covered expenses they approve when everything is settled. If you are found guilty at all, some will just void their policy with you. Unless you have an available source of a huge line of credit or several mil- lion dollars in the bank, how are you going to pay everything over several years until the case is settled and wonder if your insurance company will decide to reimburse you? You may want to carefully consider buying a Homeowners or Renters policy.

Some insurers are very comfortable offering Homeowners or Renters policy's that provide liability coverage for the use of intentional but reasonable force when protecting people (and sometimes property). Other insurers refuse to cover any intentional use of force even if it is used in your self defense. Will your insurer cover intentional acts of self defense?

First, all liability policies exclude harm you intended to or expected to inflict on others. Some policy's stop there, while other's will agree to not apply this exclusion if you were using "reasonable force" to protect yourself or others. This is called a coverage grant and is very important because the insurance company will also pay an unlimited amount for your defense costs for claims "to which this coverage applies". If the "coverage applies" you do not need to worry about how much money will you need should you injure an innocent bystander or two because your shots missed your intended target and hit someone else? I believe that properly protecting your life savings is also important.

Let's look at an insuring agreement from an actual liability section in a Homeowner's policy.

Liability Coverages

PRINCIPAL COVERAGES -- LIABILITY AND MEDICAL PAYMENTS TO OTHERS

Coverage L -- Personal Liability -- "We" pay, up to "our" "limit", all sums for which an "insured" is liable by law because of "bodily injury" or "property damage" caused by an "occurrence" to which this coverage applies. "We" will defend a suit seeking damages if the suit resulted from "bodily injury" or "property damage" not excluded under this coverage. "We" may make investigations and settle claims or suits that "we" decide are appropriate. "We" do not have to provide a defense after "we" have paid an amount equal to "our" "limit" as a result of a judgment or written settlement.

Coverage M -- Medical Payments To Others –

"We" pay the necessary medical expenses if they are incurred or medically determined within three years from the date of an accident causing "bodily injury" covered by this policy.

Sounds pretty good, right? But there is an exclusion that removes coverage for intentional acts in the policy. This exclusion needs to be excluded and provide coverage for justified acts of self defense. Here is how it's done.

Exclusions That Apply To Coverages L and M -- This policy does not apply to:

"bodily injury" or "property damage":
1) which is expected by, directed by, or intended by an "insured";
2) that is the result of a criminal act of an "insured"; or
3) that is the result of an intentional and malicious act by or at the direction of an "insured".

This exclusion applies even if:
1) the "bodily injury" or "property damage" that occurs is different than what was expected by, directed by, or intended by the "insured"; or
2) the "bodily injury" or "property damage" is suffered by someone other than the person or persons expected by, directed by, or intended by the "insured".

However, this exclusion does not apply to "bodily injury" or "property damage" that arises out of the use of reasonable force to protect people or property.*

***This sentence is called a coverage grant.** It brings back coverage for your specific use of reasonable force in self defense.

If you find a similar sentence as bolded above in your homeowners' policy, your use of reasonable force (fists, 2x4, or a gun) for self defense is a covered occurrence including the cost of your defense. Now re-read this not as an exclusion, but how you could be **insured for your liability and defense costs.**

And I have learned that most people, who switch their insurance to self defense friendly insurers, actually pay an average of about **$200 per year less** for their insurance. Your premiums will vary based upon your underwriting criteria and claims history. Because armed citizens are "certified good guys", insurers recognize this in their underwriting and often charge us lower premiums.

Please call your insurance agent today to find out if you are properly insured or not! If it turns out you are not properly insured and your agent can't seem to help you, please contact an LTI instructor or LEOSA Trainers, Inc., and we will be very happy to help you find an agent.

Timing is important. Waiting until after your gun goes bang will be too late. Take care of this important matter while you are waiting for your license to arrive in the mail.

Finding an attorney

When you need an attorney is not the best time to be looking for one. Know who you are going to call before the handgun goes bang and your defensive gun use is now in the aftermath stage.

Interview a number of attorneys, who practice criminal defense law. Skip the attorney that wrote your will, helped you buy your house or did your divorce. This is about your liberty and you need an attorney that understands criminal defense, the weapons laws of Wisconsin, and the laws of privilege and self-defense. It would be better if the attorney has a Wisconsin license to carry and carries on a regular basis. The Shooters Bar (www.theshootersbar. org), Jews for the Preservation of Firearms Ownership (www.jpfo.org/filegen-a-m/attorney.htm) or Legal Match (www.legalmatch.com) are national registries of attorney's who specialize in DGU cases and license to carry law.

And remember: A gun never solves problems.

Chapter 6
Routine Police Encounters

Most people who carry a handgun will never encounter a deadly threat or be involved with the police in a serious criminal matter. Realistically, unless on the range, most license holders will not touch their guns other than to put them on and put them away. And that is of course a good thing.

License holders will encounter police officers from time to time as everybody does. Whether it is the police officer on overtime at the local drugstore, the one who has pulled you over for an out-of-order turn signal, or sitting nearby at a restaurant having lunch.

This chapter deals with ordinary police encounters, ones where issues of deadly force, police investigations, and the threat or reality of arrest are *not* involved.

It is important to know that the Wisconsin Personal Protection Act provides for a statewide computerized registry of license holders that is available to law enforcement officers for official use only. In Wisconsin a license to carry (and appropriate ID) must be presented to a law enforcement officer upon request (Wis. Stat. 175.6(2g) (b) (c)). Failure to present a license is $25 forfeiture. The forfeiture will be dismissed if the license is produced within 48 hours to the agency that employees the requesting officer.

Do not argue

Times and places to argue with police are nearly nonexistent. The roadside is not one of them, nor are other routine encounters. Not arguing does not mean agreeing. Keeping any interaction with police on a pleasant and professional level makes any encounter go better for the officer and you.

Police are human beings. They come to work wanting to go home alive and well. Officers are now being challenged to interact with law abiding armed citizens. They must develop or refine their skills of determining who is a wolf and who is a fellow sheepdog. For some, this is not going to be difficult. For a few this will be an uncomfortable adjustment.

When to display your license

Under the Wisconsin PPA, a license holder has no general obligation to inform a police officer that he or she is armed, *unless* asked.

If asked, there is no option: you must display your license and photo identification.

While people new to carrying a handgun assume that everybody has X-ray vision and can spot the gun immediately that is simply not the case. If the contact is casual and amounts to no more than an exchange of pleasantries then displaying your license to an officer raise a concern.

If the contact is based on official business, you have the choice of voluntarily displaying your license to the officer before he asks. We have found that informing the officer demonstrates your concern for the officer's safety and comfort. Chalk it up to living the "Golden Rule." You could be pleasantly surprised at the outcome.

Informing the officer you are a license holder voluntarily is a good idea should the contact involve the discovery of your handgun. Surprising an officer on duty Christmas morning with coffee and a donut is one thing. Surprising an officer at the mall with the handgun he did not expect to see is another matter. If your contact is heading anywhere near your handgun just say; "I have a license to carry and I am armed." The officer may ask further questions or may just say "thanks for letting me know."

Here is a tip. Learn to carry your weapons license and ID opposite from your handgun. You will lessen the concern of accessing your license if it is not next to your handgun

It should go without saying no mention of your license is necessary unless you are asked.

Be polite

Consider the concern that a police officer may have, particularly during the new carry law "break-in" period, when he or she has rarely if ever encountered a law-abiding armed citizen. Some officers are going to be nervous, and while there is no need to be overly familiar, simple politeness will help to reassure the officer that you are not going to be a problem, whether the handgun issue comes up or not.

In many ways, the success of Wisconsin's carry law is in understanding and appreciating the issues of all involved. License holders do not deserve or want to be harassed. Law enforcement officers want and deserve to be safe in the company of license holders. The general public expects that license holders and law enforcement officers all both respect the law.

Obey all instructions promptly

This should be obvious but, If you are confused, politely ask for clarification. When you are obeying instructions, *say* what you are doing, "I'm getting my wallet out now, as you have told me," for example. Make it clear that you are cooperating with the officer's commands.

The instructions you will be obeying have to do with physical actions. Providing information (ID, carry license, proof of insurance, registration) necessary for the business at hand can and should be produced.

It is important to understand the difference between consensual police contact, lawfully detaining you temporarily, and arrest.

- Consensual contact allows you to walk away at any time.
- Lawfully detaining contact for investigative purposes is a Terry stop, which requires the officer to have an articulable suspicion based upon the totality of the circumstances that a crime has been, is being, or is about to be committed. Although you are temporarily not free to

leave, you are not required to answer questions beyond providing identification if asked.
- Arrest is when you have lost your liberty. You are not free to leave. Loss of liberty does not necessarily begin when you are told you are under arrest.   It can begin well before you are read your Miranda rights.

Maintain control of your weapon

Almost invariably when a police officer decides to take possession of your handgun the officer will choose to retrieve it himself. That is what they are trained to do. If you are asked to relinquish control of the handgun kindly decline by saying, "I don't consent to any seizure." The officer can take possession of your handgun under a Terry stop. The WPPA is silent regarding when and how to return the handgun to the licensee. It is likely to be based on the facts of the situation. That said, without any evidence or facts tying the license holder to the "reasonable articulable suspicion" that is the basis for the Terry stop, the firearm should be returned once the contact is complete.

Do not offer to turn over your handgun before the officer asks you to do so, because you do not want to give up your Fourth Amendment rights by "consenting" to a search or seizure.

Should your gun be seized, ask for a receipt. The law requires a receipt to be issued; however, some officers do not remember this.

Keep your hands in plain sight

This should be largely common sense. The idea is not to make the police officer nervous, and they can, even in ordinary confrontations, become very nervous about things like quick movements and hands in pockets. As they say, "cops love to see hands."

Do not consent to a search or seizure

Police officers will, from time to time, ask your permission to search you or your car. Proactively inform officers that you do not consent to any search or seizure. As a general rule do not answer police questions with a "yes" or "no." "You don't mind if I look in your care do you?" This question is phrased so it cannot be answered by a simple yes or no without giving your permission. That does not mean, of course, that you will not be searched: just do not consent to one.

Legally speaking, a full search is different from being "patted down" or a "pat-down search." A pat-down search is just what it sounds like: the police officer pats on your clothes attempting to see if you have a weapon. They do not get to stick their hands inside your clothes or pockets unless they feel a weapon through the garment.

Often police officers want to search people they stop, even for minor traffic offenses. But if there is not "an articulable suspicion based upon the totality of the circumstances that a crime has been, is being, or is about to be committed" they cannot even pat you down —unless they ask you for permission and you say "yes."

So do not. Just politely say, "I do not consent to any search or seizure." Do not consent to a search of your car, either. Many people we know have refused consent, and the police officers simply turned to other matters. They knew that saying no was a matter of right and were not offended.

If you are asked to consent to a search and you refuse the officer may not be happy. He may tell you that he can make you wait there until he gets a search warrant or they may call a dog to sniff the car. Most likely that will not happen. The fact that you do not give permission for him to search your car is not enough evidence to persuade a judge to issue a search warrant.

Most likely, he'll finish writing the ticket and send you on your way.

When a routine encounter becomes something else

It is possible what began as a routine police encounter becomes something more. This can happen without any warning and without you necessarily having done something wrong, or done anything at all.

When a routine encounter becomes non-routine, it is necessary for you to immediately transition into a defensive mode and behave just as you would after a situation where you had used, or threatened to use, deadly force. For that, go back to the chapter *Lethal Force and its Aftermath.*

When the encounter turns sour immediately lawyer up. Do not wait, there is no downside to immediately saying, "I need to talk to my lawyer, and I do not consent to any search or seizure."

At the end of the day

Police officers want and deserve to be safe in the company of license holders. The general public wants to know that license holders and law enforcement both respect the law.

Over time police officers and sheep will learn that armed citizens pose no threat to them. They will learn that we are some of their biggest supporters and strongest allies. Wolves will also gain a healthy respect for license holders! License holders must be willing to take the time for this learning curve to take place. It is a process and you can help everyone become more comfortable with having armed citizens in the community.

And remember: a gun never solves problems.

Chapter 7
Choosing a Handgun for Carry

This chapter is like writing an advice for the lovelorn column. No matter what your problem is, or the advice we may offer, there will always be someone who thinks our advice is wrong or that they have the better answer for you. That is just the nature of this subject. Quite frankly because there are so many different people it is also the reason why there are so many different types and sizes of handguns.

Our objective in this chapter is not to tell you what handgun you should or should not buy, but to instruct you how to determine for yourself what is the best handgun for you.

We would like to offer at least several unvarnished universal truths about the handgun you decide to carry, no matter what make or caliber it is, or if it is a semiautomatic or a revolver.

- Every time you press the trigger, it must go bang.
- The performance of any cartridge is dictated by physics and apply equally to any bullet while in flight.
- Penetration is dictated by bullet weight, impact, velocity and expanded diameter. Generally, when different bullets penetrate to the same depth those moving faster and exhibit the largest expansion will damage the most tissue.
- A gun will not get lighter as the day goes on.
- If a handgun does not fit you, you cannot competently shoot it.

The most important characteristic for a good choice in a handgun that you will carry to protect your life, is that it must be reliable in order to protect your life. Reliable and expensive are not interchangeable terms, but it is likely that a reliable quality handgun will cost more than one that is not so reliable. To determine your budget, ask yourself how much money are you willing to spend on a handgun that will be expected to save your life?

If you have done any prior internet research about what is a good handgun to carry, you are probably more confused now than when you began. It is difficult to ask ten people about what they think would be a good carry gun and expect any two answers to be even close to the same advice. So if you do not typically ask your friends or a total stranger to help you decide what shoes you should buy, our advice is stop asking others what handgun you should buy as well. Just like shoes, you need to decide what is the right handgun for you based upon how often you will wear your handgun, how it fits your own body, how comfortable it is to use, how it will work with your wardrobe, how much it will cost, how you intend to carry it and other personal factors.

First, from a purely mechanical standpoint you can choose between either a revolver or a semiautomatic. Although there is other technology available such as a derringer, they are not as well suited for your personal protection as they are for poker players in old western movies. Revolvers and semiautomatics both have advantages and disadvantages which we will discuss. Your job is to decide for yourself which type of handgun will suite you the best.

We would like to remind you that your carry gun will be a working gun. It is going to live with you and go wherever you go. It will soon show some wear and tear and you can expect it to get dirty and dusty and rusty just from your wearing it all the time.

You should also search for holsters that are commercially available for the handgun that you would like to carry before you decide to spend a substantial amount on your new gun, only to learn there are only a few holsters available that it will fit. Custom holsters can be made for any gun, but they will generally be much more expensive than one that is commercially made. No matter where or how you decide to carry your handgun, for your safety it must always be carried in a holster! No exceptions.

Revolvers

Revolvers have been compared to mans' best friend, a dog. Revolvers are reliable, they bark when you press the trigger every time. They are not complicated pieces of machinery and are certainly not high maintenance. They are not fussy about the ammunition that you feed them, but they generally have a more limited supply of ammunition. Revolvers  shoot ammunition that is normally more powerful than semiautomatics so fewer shots may be needed to stop a threat (it is still shot placement and the amount of tissue destroyed that matters the most to stop a threat). However, because revolvers do not use any of the recoil to operate, you will feel all of the recoil of the more powerful rounds against your hands and arms, which can make them more uncomfortable for you to shoot.

Because revolvers can be more challenging to use, they are generally carried by the more experienced shooters. The wider physical size of the cylinders and/or the revolvers larger grip can make them a bit more difficult to carry concealed when carried on your hip. A solution to carrying a physically larger handgun concealed may be to buy a shoulder holster which will tuck your handgun more closely to your body and under your arm.

Small frame .38 Special revolvers are commonly carried in a front pocket. If you buy a revolver to carry in a pocket, be sure it has an enclosed

hammer which will enable you to draw it from your pocket without the hammer snagging on your clothing or catching on your key ring.

Small frame revolvers are also a good choice to carry as a backup gun in an ankle holster. You could carry either your pocket revolver or a revolver with an exposed hammer in an ankle holster.

Advances in metallurgy have made it possible to manufacture very strong but lightweight handguns. The fall of the Soviet Union has allowed

firearms manufacturers access to Scandium which comes from areas that were once behind the iron curtain, which when added to aluminum, makes it suitable for use in handguns.

The main application of scandium by weight is in aluminum scandium alloys for minor aerospace industry components. These alloys contain between 0.1% and 0.5% of scandium. They were used in the Russian military aircraft, specifically the MiG-21 and MiG-29.

Some sports equipment which relies on high performance materials such as baseball bats, and bicycle frames have been made with scandium-aluminum alloys. Lacrosse sticks

are also made with scandium-titanium alloys to take advantage of the strength of titanium.

Smith & Wesson produces revolvers and pistols with frames composed of scandium alloy and cylinders of titanium chambered in .38 Special and .357 Magnum. These lightweight handguns are considerably more comfortable and more accurate to shoot when using lower pressure ammunition instead of full pressure magnum rounds. With scandium alloy light weight revolvers, it is very important to buy ammunition made specifically for these guns. Although they will shoot full pressure ammunition, you will not appreciate the results. Because scandium is a very rare metal, the price of a handgun that is made with it will be much more than a similar model made from steel.

A newer caliber of .327 Magnum has been designed as an alternative to the more challenging .357 Magnum. The advantages of this revolver are that the ballistics of a .327 Magnum are very similar to that of a .357 Magnum, however the revolver handles much more like a less powerful .32 Magnum. It delivers the punch you need without the pain (to you anyway).

Because the grip does not also have to contain the ammunition within it, a revolver offers a much wider array of options to properly size to your hand. A large grip may be replaced with a smaller grip or a smaller grip may be replaced with a larger grip on the same revolver.

Semiautomatics

Semiautomatics are more like cats than dogs. They are more complicated pieces of machinery, and they are more susceptible to failure to fire at the worst possible time. They can and will jam.

Like a cat, a semiautomatic may not like the ammunition you feed it, although most do have a higher ammunition capacity than a revolver.

Semiautomatics do require more maintenance more often to keep them working.

Most people do prefer to carry a semiautomatic instead of a revolver. Even a higher caliber semiautomatic such as the .45 ACP, is easier to shoot than a smaller caliber revolver. First, the recoil of a semiautomatics smaller cartridge is less than a revolver cartridge and secondly, the semiautomatic absorbs some of the energy from the recoil to operate itself and prepare itself for the next round to be shot (this why the term "semiautomatic" is used to describe these handguns). We train new shooters to shoot with a semiautomatic and people then become comfortable with this technology from the early stages of their shooting experience. We are all creatures of habit and people often stay with what they are familiar with and comfortable using.

Ammunition is generally less expensive for semiautomatics, which makes the cost of regularly practicing with them more affordable for the average person. There is also a vast assortment of ammunition in each caliber to appease those finicky semi automatics. We would caution you against choosing a caliber such as a 10mm or .357 Sig because ammunition for these calibers is not as commonly available as .380 ACP, 9mm, .40 Cal and .45 ACP ammunition at retailers or gun ranges.

Have you ever wondered why some handguns seem right for you and others are very difficult to shoot or do not operate for you as you expect? Have you ever shot a handgun knowing you were aiming dead center of the target and your shot ended up to either to the left or right of the bulls eye? Have you experienced your shots hitting the target far from where you thought you were aiming? Has a friend loaned you their gun to shoot that they were very proficient shooting but you could not hit the broad side of a barn from the inside with it?

Fitting a gun

People are inclined to blame the gun for these issues and if you did, you would be half right. The other half of the blame is your hand. These issues happen when the gun does not fit your hand correctly and therefore you cannot operate the handgun correctly. This is what we refer to as a classic train wreck of a relationship. If you happen to own a handgun that you cannot shoot correctly because it is the wrong gun for you, sell it because the gun is not going to change its size and neither is your hand. This is also the primary reason that well intended advice which gun you should buy from everyone else fails for you, unless you happen to get the advice from someone who is exactly the same physical size as you are. The same is true if there is one handgun in your home and you share it with someone else, unless you are the same size one of you will not be equally competent using the same handgun.

How well a handgun fits you is really as important as reliability. Even if your handgun fires every time you press the trigger but all of your shots miss your intended target, you are in big trouble. Shooting innocent people because you cannot control your handgun is unacceptable and very expensive. Failing to stop your attacker could cost you your life.

Do not expect the guy behind the counter at the gun store to be very helpful. Gun store people are usually very knowledgeable about the technical features of a good number of firearms, but most of them are not trained to know how to fit a gun to you correctly.

As we have mentioned, fitting handguns and shoes are very similar. They both need a correct width (grip) and length (frame) to fit you properly. For example if a shoe is too short or too narrow for you, it is too small and you cannot put it on or if you do your foot will soon hurt you. If it is too long or too wide, it is too large and your foot will float around inside your shoe and your foot will develop blisters. Neither your feet nor your shoes will ever adjust their size to each other so your shoes will never fit you comfortably. Wearing the shoes more often will not resolve the problem just like practicing with a gun that does not fit you will not correct your shooting problems either. Make sense?

To perform a handgun fitting procedure you may need a mirror or a trusting friend to help you determine the fit of your handgun selections.

<u>Before you do anything with a handgun, perform a clearing procedure to verify that it is unloaded.</u>

The first measurement you need to make is the grip. Every time you pick up a handgun, your strong side (shooting hand) knuckles should automatically land directly below the trigger guard. No adjustment should be necessary to align your knuckles where they  belong. If your knuckles are off to the side of the trigger guard, this means the grip is either too large or too small for your hand. Some firearms do have grip options you can try to help you adjust the grip size however the magazine well on a semi automatic is not adjustable. If the gun still does not fit your hand by changing to another grip option, the grip will never fit you correctly. You are holding the wrong gun. Try again with another handgun. Keep track of the price of each handgun you try out that does not fit you. This is the running total of the money you are saving.

Once you have found a handgun with a correct grip size for you, the second measurement and an equally important one is the length or frame size. To determine this measurement, with the action at rest (firearm verified as unloaded, hammer not cocked, the safety off and the muzzle pointed in a safe direction) gently touch the trigger but do not press it. Every time you touch the trigger, your  trigger finger should always land on the trigger half way between the tip of your finger and first joint. No adjustment should be necessary. If your finger cannot reach in far enough, this means the frame is too large. If your finger goes in too far and the trigger is near the first joint of your finger, this means the frame is too small. If your finger does not land half way between the tip and first joint, you will either push or pull the barrel every time you

 shoot because your finger does not land correctly on the trigger. Correct finger placement on the trigger is very important because when your finger touches the trigger correctly, when you press the trigger it will come straight back and not change the direction of the barrel as you shoot the handgun.

This fitting process is identical for both a revolver and a semi automatic handgun.

Once you know a particular handgun correctly fits your hand, measure the distance between the top knuckle directly below the trigger guard of your shooting hand and the bottom of your trigger finger as you touch the trigger. You can mark this distance with a pen or a pencil. You just need to know the distance. Once you have this information you can pick up any handgun and if the grip size is correct, you can easily measure the frame size and immediately tell if the handgun you are holding fits you and will shoot correctly for you or not.

A gun that does not fit you correctly cannot be shot by you accurately, just like shoes that do not fit you correctly cannot be worn by you comfortably.

Okay, by now there should be a pile of handguns in front of you that all fit you. If you touched enough guns at the gun store, you might realize that one consideration is of little importance when fitting a handgun, caliber. But the caliber is still an important part of your decision when choosing the right handgun for you.

In fact, you may have a variety of calibers from which you can choose. Make a list of the make and model of all these guns and take your list to a range where you can rent these guns before you decide which one to buy. You will be deciding what is the correct caliber for you at the gun range. You need to buy some ammunition for each gun that you have determined fits you so you can see how competent you are shooting it. The right caliber for you will be the largest caliber that you can accurately shoot center of mass (within the largest middle area) of a silhouette target set at 21 feet, without using the guns sights. This is called point shooting and is what you will naturally do when you are under an attack. All your shots must be placed on the silhouette, with no shots missing the target completely or in the white paper area around the silhouette. You want to buy the handgun that you achieve the best grouping of rounds with the largest caliber.

> Here is a shooting tip to help you tighten your shots into a smaller group; push forward with your shooting hand as you pull back with your non-shooting shooting hand and clamp the handgun in your palm. The harder you clamp the gun, the less the gun will move and your shots will be closer together.

We do not know which handgun(s) will be right for you. What is important is that you will know which handgun(s) will be right for you when you are finished shooting. You may learn that you are equally competent with more than one handgun. That is okay. If your budget allows, give them all a good home.

And remember: A gun never solves problems.

82

CHAPTER 8
The Wisconsin Personal Protection Act

Before turning to the details of the mechanics of carrying a handgun in public it is necessary to review applicable state, federal laws and DOJ regulations with particular attention to the new Wisconsin weapons law. The legislature failed to give Wisconsin's new weapons law a name.

Those of us who work with it on a regular basis have named it the *Wisconsin Personal Protection Act* ("WPPA"). The law amended a number of Wisconsin statutes and created a few new ones affecting constitutional carry and created a license to carry certain weapons concealed; prohibiting certain acts and prescribing certain penalties. It is a major change and is largely contained in Section 175.60 of Wisconsin statutes. The full act is contained in appendix B.

All the changes to carrying a weapon in Wisconsin are predicated on the lawful possession of a weapon and specifically a firearm. Immediately below are the long and somewhat arduous state and federal statutes regarding possession of a firearm courtesy of the Wisconsin Attorney general's office. Enjoy!

Under state law the following persons are prohibited from possessing a firearm. Firearms possession laws are generally found in (Wis. Stat. 941.29). In addition to persons a court has ordered as a condition of release on bail to be prohibited from possessing a dangerous weapon, a person is prohibited under (Wis. Stat. 941.29(1) and (2) from possessing a firearm if any of the following apply:

1. The person has been convicted of a felony in Wisconsin. (Wis. Stat. 941.29(1)(a)). Unless the person has been pardoned of the felony and has been expressly authorized to possess a firearm under 18 USC app. 1203; or has been relieved of disabilities under 18 USC 925(c). (Wis. Stat. 941.29(5)).

2. The person has been convicted of a crime elsewhere that would be a felony if convicted in Wisconsin. (Wis. Stat. 941.29(1)(b)). Unless the person has been pardoned of the felony and has been expressly authorized to possess a firearm under 18 USC app. 1203; or has been relieved of disabilities under 18 USC 925(c). (Wis. Stat. 941.29(5).

3. The person was adjudicated delinquent for an act committed on or after April 21, 1994, that if committed by an adult in this state would be a felony. (Wis. Stat. 941.29(1)(bm)). Unless a court subsequently determines that the person is not likely to act in a manner dangerous to public safety. (Wis. Stat. 941.29(8)).

4. The person was found not guilty of a felony in Wisconsin by reason of mental disease or defect. (Wis. Stat § 941.29(1)(c)). Unless, a court subsequently determines that: 1) the person is no longer insane or no longer has a mental disease, defect or illness, AND 2) the person is not likely to act in a manner dangerous to public safety. (Wis. Stat. § 941.29(7)).

5. The person was found not guilty or not responsible for a crime elsewhere that would be a felony in this state by reason of insanity or mental illness, disease or defect. (Wis. Stat. 941.29(1)(d)). Unless, a court subsequently determines that: 1) the person is no longer insane or no longer has a mental disease, defect or illness, AND 2) the person is not likely to act in a manner dangerous to public safety. (Wis. Stat. § 941.29(7)).

6. The person has been committed to treatment under (Wis.

Stat. 51.20(13)(a)) and ordered not to possess a firearm under (Wis. Stat. 51.20(13(cv)1). (Wis. Stat. 941.29(1)(e)). Unless the prohibition has been cancelled. (Wis. Stat. 941.20(9)(a)).

7. The person has been ordered not to possess a firearm under any of (Wis. Stat. 51.20(13)(cv)1, 51.45(13)(i)1, 54.10(3)(f)1, or 55.12(10)(a) (mental health commitments)). (Wis. Stat. 941.20(1) (em)). Unless the court order has been cancelled. (Wis. Stat. 941.20(9b)).

8. The person is enjoined under an injunction issued under (Wis. Stat. 813.12 or 813.122 (harassment or domestic abuse)) or under a tribal injunction, as defined in (Wis. Stat. 813.12(1)(e)), issued by a court established by any federally recognized Wisconsin Indian tribe or band, except the Menominee Indian tribe of Wisconsin, that includes notice to the respondent that he or she is subject to the requirements and penalties under § 941.29 and that has been filed under (Wis. Stat. 806.247(3)). (Wis. Stat. 941.29(1)(f)). Unless the person is a peace officer and the person possesses a firearm while in the line of duty or, if required to do so as a condition of employment, while off duty; OR, 2) the person is a member of the U.S. armed forces or national guard and the person possesses a firearm while in the line of duty. (Wis. Stat. 941.29(10)).

Under federal law the following persons are prohibited from possessing a firearm that has been shipped or transported in interstate or foreign commerce, or possess in or affecting commerce, any firearm or ammunition; or to receive any firearm or ammunition which has been shipped or transported in interstate or foreign commerce. 18 USC Ch. 44 922(g)(1)-(9).

1   A person who has been convicted in any court of, a crime punishable by imprisonment for a term exceeding one year;

2. A person who is a fugitive from justice;

3. A person who is an unlawful user of or addicted to any controlled substance (as defined in section 102 of the Controlled Substances Act (21 U.S.C. 802));

4. A person who has been adjudicated as a mental defective or who has been committed to a mental institution;

5. A person who, being an alien—
   (A) is illegally or unlawfully in the United States; or
   (B) except as provided in subsection 18 USC 44 § 922(y)(2), has been admitted to the United States under a nonimmigrant visa (as that term is defined in section 101(a)(26) of the Immigration and Nationality Act (8 U.S.C. 1101 (a)(26));
6. A person who has been discharged from the Armed Forces under dishonorable conditions;
7. A person who, having been a citizen of the United States, has renounced person represents a credible threat to the physical safety of such intimate partner or child; or
   (ii) by its terms explicitly prohibits the use, attempted use, or threatened use of physical force against such intimate partner or child that would reasonably be expected to cause bodily injury his or her citizenship;
8. A person who is subject to a court order that—
   (A) was issued after a hearing of which such person received actual notice, and at which such person had an opportunity to participate;
   (B) restrains such person from harassing, stalking, or threatening an intimate partner of such person or child of such intimate partner or person, or engaging in other conduct that would place an intimate partner in reasonable fear of bodily injury to the partner or child; and
   (C) (i) includes a finding that such A person who has been convicted in any court of, a crime punishable by imprisonment for a term exceeding one year;
9. A person who has been convicted in any court of a misdemeanor crime of domestic violence.

(The above legal citations are taken from the Wisconsin Attorney Generals FAQ on Wisconsin's new concealed weapons law dated 8/1/11).

Under both federal and Wisconsin state law there are several avenues for the reinstatement of the right to possess a firearm. Consult with an attorney regarding reinstatement opportunities.

Obtaining a License

Once you have passed a training course, or have any of the other approved documentation demonstrating training, the next step is to apply for your carry license. The application form is available on line at the Wisconsin Department of Justice website and once completed can be submitted by mail or other means made available by the DOJ.

The submission must include:

1. A completed application form. The forms shall require the applicant to provide only his or her name, address, date of birth, state identification card number, race, sex, height, and eye color and shall include all of the following statements.
2. A statement that the applicant is ineligible for a license if any of the following applies:
    i.   The individual is less than 21 years of age.
    ii.   The individual is prohibited under federal law from possessing a firearm that has been transported in interstate or foreign commerce.
    iii. The individual is prohibited from possessing a firearm under s. 941.29.
    iv.   The court has prohibited the individual from possessing a dangerous weapon under state law. (Wis Stat. 969.02 (3) (c) or 969.03 (1) (c)).
    v.   The individual is on release under (Wis. Stat. 969.01) and the individual may not possess a dangerous weapon as a condition of the release.
    vi.   The individual is not a Wisconsin resident.
    vii. The individual has not provided proof of training as described under sub. (4)(a).
3. A statement explaining self-defense and defense of others under (Wis. Stat. 939.48), with a place for the applicant to sign his or her name to indicate that he or she has read and understands the statement.
4. A statement, with a place for the applicant to sign his or her name, to indicate that the applicant has read and understands the requirements of this section (Wis. stat. 175.60).
5. A statement that an applicant may be prosecuted if he or

she intentionally gives a false answer to any question on the application or intentionally submits a falsified document with the application.

6. A statement of the penalties for intentionally giving a false answer to any question on the application or intentionally submitting a falsified document with the application.

7. A statement of the places where a licensee is prohibited from carrying a weapon, as well as an explanation of the provisions that could limit the places where the licensee may carry a weapon under (Wis. Stat. 175.60(16), 175.60(1m), 943.13 (1m)(c) and 948.605(2)(b)1r) with a place for the applicant to sign his or her name to indicate that he or she has read and understands the statement.

8. A statement that states that the information that he or she is providing in the application submitted and any document submitted with the application is true and complete to the best of his or her knowledge.

9. A license fee in an amount, as determined by the department by rule, that is equal to the cost of issuing the license but does not exceed $37.

10. A fee for a background check that is equal to the fee charged under (Wis. Stat. 175.35 (2i)).

11. Proof of training as described under sub. (4)(a).

Reciprocity and recognition

Reciprocity means Wisconsin and another state formally agree to recognize each other's carry licenses. Recognition means Wisconsin voluntarily recognizes the carry license of another state even if the other state does not recognize Wisconsin's carry license. Other state's laws determine if they may enable the state to recognize Wisconsin's carry license. Generally, a state's Attorney General's office or

Department of Public Safety will maintain a list of carry licenses that state recognizes.

The WPPA authorized the Department of Justice to enter into reciprocity agreements with other states regarding carrying a firearm. The statute also provides the criteria for the DOJ to recognize other states carry licenses for those that are at least 21 years of age.

Remember when carrying a handgun in another state under a Wisconsin weapons license or any other states license or permit to carry a firearm you are required to follow the laws of the state in which you are standing. Conversely, out of state licensees must follow Wisconsin's laws. State laws can vary widely as to what is legal or not legal. Forewarned is forearmed.

A Wisconsin resident may hold as many out of state licenses as they care too. They will have to go through whatever hoops each state requires to attain those licenses. In some cases, merely holding a Wisconsin License is sufficient to attain a out-of-state license Other states may require additional training. Generally, the more licenses held by a person the more states they can carry in. History has proven that states change, without notice, what states carry licenses they honor.

Scope of license

Individual limitations on your license to carry are not allowed. The DOJ cannot impose any unique restrictions upon a licensee. State law prevents local jurisdictions from enacting local ordinances that are not the same or substantially similar to state law. So, your license is good border to border.

- A license to carry a concealed weapon issued under this section shall meet the requirements established by the legislature.
- The department may not impose conditions, limitations, or requirements that are not expressly provided for in this section on the issuance, scope, effect, or content of a license.
- Unless expressly provided in this section, this section does not limit an individual's right to carry a firearm that is not concealed.

For purposes of 18 USC 922 an out-of-state licensee is considered licensed by Wisconsin. This is important so that out-of-state licensees will be exempted from the state and federal restrictions regarding 1000 feet school zones.

Display of license

Constitutional (unlicensed) open carry of a handgun remains legal in Wisconsin. A licensee or out-of-state licensee may carry their handgun openly or concealed. Open carry, not being prohibited, may draw closer law enforcement attention to you.

Unless the licensee or out-of-state licensee is carrying a concealed weapon in his or her own dwelling or place of business, or on land that he or she owns, leases, or otherwise legally occupies, a licensee or out-of-state licensee shall have with him or her his or her license document and photographic identification card and an out-of-state licensee shall have with him or her his or her out-of-state license and photographic identification card at all times during which he or she is carrying a weapon.

A licensee or out-of-state licensee who is in public and carrying a concealed weapon shall display his or her license document and photographic identification card to a requesting law enforcement officer. Someone not carrying their license and photographic ID when asked may be required to forfeit not more than $25. If the person presents, within 48 hours, his or her license document or out-of-state license and photographic identification to the law enforcement agency that employs the requesting law enforcement officer the forfeiture is waived. This applies only if carrying a weapon concealed or not constitutionally carrying. (Wis. Stat.175.6(2g)(c))

School Zones

For whatever reason, legislators and school administrators throughout the United States cannot bring themselves to understand that gun free school zones are a greater danger to students than are licensed armed citizens. Wisconsin is no different.

It is a class I felony for anyone to be in or on the grounds of a school (1-12) with a firearm.

The law differentiates between licensees and non-licensees as to the 1000 foot zone around the grounds of a school. Non-licensee must remain outside the 1000 foot school zone when armed or face a class B forfeiture ($1000). There are some exceptions for those who reside within the 1000 foot zone or lawfully transporting their firearm through the school zone.

Licensees may carry within the 1000 foot school zone. Licensees may NOT carry on school grounds, not even on school parking lots.

Universities and Colleges operate under the posting section of the WPPA and both private and public are treated the same. Anyone who is armed and enters or remains in any privately or publicly owned building on the grounds of a university or college, is guilty of a class B forfeiture ($1000), if the university or college has notified the citizens not to enter or remain in the building while carrying a firearm or with that type of firearm. This provision does not apply to a person who leases residential or business premises in the building.

Under a separate statute, dangerous weapons (other than a firearm, BB or pellet gun) are prohibited in or on any school building, school grounds, recreation area, athletic field or any other property owned, used or operated for school administration. So although electronic control devices, knives and billy clubs are not specifically prohibited under the WPPA, they are covered under separate statute (Wis. Stat. 948.61.)), with the exception cited below (Wis. Stat. 948.61(3)(e)).

School is defined as a public, parochial or private, or tribal school that provides educational programs for one or more grades between grades 1 and 12 (elementary, middle, junior high and high school). (Wis. Stat. 948.61(1)(b)).

As with most laws there are some exceptions. Below are exceptions to the prohibition on possessing dangerous weapons on school premises by the following persons:

- A person who uses a weapon solely for school sanctioned purposes. (Wis. Stat. 948.61(3)(a)).
- A person who engages in military activities sponsored by the federal or state government when acting in the discharge of his or her official duties. (Wis. Stat. § 948.61(3)(b)).
- A person who is a law enforcement officer or state certified commission warden acting in the discharge of his or her official duties. (Wis. Stat. 948.61(3)(c)).
- A person who is participating in a convocation authorized by school authorities in which weapons of collectors or instructors are handled or displayed. (Wis. Stat. 948.61(3)(d)).
- A person who drives a motor vehicle in which a dangerous weapon is located onto school premises for school sanctioned purposes or for the purpose of delivering or picking up passengers or property if the weapon is not removed from the vehicle or used in any way. (Wis. Stat. 948.61(3)(e)).
- A person who possesses or uses a bow and arrow or knife while legally hunting in a school forest if the school board has decided that hunting may be allowed in the school forest. (Wis. Stat. 948.61(3)(f)).

Posted places

Generally speaking, that which is not *specifically prohibited* is allowed. A license holder can carry a handgun most places, including public places, except where specifically prohibited by law or by proper notice from the property owner or lawful occupant. The posting provision only applies to firearms or a particular type of firearm. Electronic control devices, billy clubs or knives (other than switchblades) are not mentioned by the posting section of the law. Since these weapons are not specifically authorized to be prohibited under the posting section they appear to be allowed. Posting language begins at (Wis. Stat. 943.13(1e)(h) and 943.13(1m) (c).

Parking facilities

Here is the good news. Unless otherwise prohibited (for example 1- 12 schools) an armed citizen may store a firearm in their vehicle when parked in a private or public parking facility. We will mention any parking facility exceptions as we cover that type of building or location.

Residences (single family)

While carrying a firearm, enters or remains at a residence that the armed citizen does not own or occupy after the owner or leasee of the residence has given notice not to remain with a firearm, including the residence and the parcel of land upon which the residence is located. Notice can be given personally either orally or in writing.

Multi-unit residences

Individual tenants or unit owners may post their leased or owned units. Owners of the common area and grounds may post the common area and grounds. For a condominium property the board of directors of the owners association may post the common areas and grounds depending the authority granted to the board by the associations governing documents. Parking facilities (except for 1-12 school parking lots) may not be posted.

Nonresidential buildings & grounds

While carrying a firearm, enters or remains in any part of a nonresidential building, grounds of a nonresidential building, or land that the armed citizen does not own or lawfully occupy after the owner or lawful occupant of the building, grounds, or land, has notified the armed citizen not to enter or remain in that part of the building, grounds, or land while carrying a firearm (or with that type of firearm).

Nonresidential buildings include a nursing home, a community-based residential facility, a residential care apartment complex, an adult family home, and a hospice.

Government buildings

Enters or remains in any part of a building that is owned, occupied, or controlled by the state or any local governmental unit, excluding any building or portion of a building that are expressly prohibited (see prohibited places), if the state or local governmental unit has notified the armed citizen not to enter or remain in the building while carrying a firearm (or with that type of firearm). This provision does not apply to a person who leases residential or business premises in the building. Parking facilities may not be posted.

Special events

While carrying a firearm enters or remains at a special event if the organizers of the special event have notified the armed citizen not to enter or remain at the special event while carrying a firearm (or with that type of firearm. The parking facility cannot be posted.

Prohibited places

Despite the general provision that licenses to carry pistols are valid statewide, pistols or other firearms are nevertheless restricted or not allowed in the following places:

- Any portion of a building that is a police station, sheriff's office, state patrol station, or the office of a division of criminal investigation special agent of the department
- Any portion of a building that is a prison, jail, house of correction, or secured correctional facility
- The facility established under s. 46.055. (Sand Ridge Secure Treatment Center, any secured portion of a mental health facility)
- The center established under s. 46.056. (Wisconsin Resource Center)

- Any secured unit or secured portion of a mental health institute under s. 51.05, including a facility designated as the Maximum Security Facility at Mendota Mental Health Institute.
- Any portion of a building that is a county, state, or federal courthouse
- Any portion of a building that is a municipal courtroom if court is in session
- A place beyond a security checkpoint in an airport

The prohibitions do not apply to any of the following:
- A weapon in a vehicle driven or parked in a parking facility located in a building that is used as, or any portion of which is used as, a location listed above
- A weapon in a courthouse or courtroom if a judge who is a licensee is carrying the weapon or if another licensee or out-of-state licensee, whom a judge has permitted in writing to carry a weapon, is carrying the weapon.
- A weapon in a courthouse or courtroom if a district attorney, or an assistant district attorney, who is a licensee is carrying the weapon. Additionally, firearms are not permitted in federal court facilities or other federal facilities (Title 18 U.S.C. ' 930). This is just one of many federal laws regulating firearms. Federal law must also be consulted to ensure compliance with all applicable state firearm laws.

Notification

A person is considered to have received notice from the owner or occupant if he or she has been notified personally, either orally or in writing, or if the land is posted. Land is considered to be posted under this paragraph under either of the following procedures. For all of the following, "sign" means a sign that states a restriction imposed that is at least 5 inches by 7 inches.
- An owner of a multi-unit residence posted a sign that is located in a prominent place near all of the entrances to the part of the building to which the restriction applies or near all probable access points to the grounds to which the restriction applies and any individual entering the building or the grounds can be reasonably expected to see the sign.

- An owner or occupant of a part of a nonresidential building, the state or a local governmental unit, or a university or a college has notified an individual by posting a sign that is located in a prominent place near all of the entrances to the part of the building to which the restriction applies and any individual entering the building can be reasonably expected to see the sign.
- An owner or occupant of the grounds of a nonresidential building or of land has notified an individual if the owner or occupant has posted a sign that is located in a prominent place near all probable access points to the grounds or land to which the restriction applies and any individual entering the grounds or land can be reasonably expected to see the sign.
- The organizers of the special event have notified an individual if the organizers have posted a sign that is located in a prominent place near all of the entrances to the special event and any individual attending the special event can be reasonably expected to see the sign.
- The posting of land requires two (2) 11 inch square signs for every 40 acres that are conspicuously placed. Signs must state the name of the person giving notice followed by "owner" or "occupant" and an appropriate notice of the restriction.

Immunity

A person who does not prohibit an individual from carrying a concealed weapon on property that the person owns or occupies is immune from any liability arising from their decision.

An employer that does not prohibit one or more employees from carrying a concealed weapon is immune from any liability arising from that decision.

Employer restrictions

An employer may prohibit a licensee that it employs from carrying a concealed weapon or a particular type of concealed weapon in the course of the licensee's employment or during any part of the licensee's course of employment.

An employer may not prohibit a licensee, as a condition of employment, from carrying a concealed weapon, a particular type of concealed weapon, or ammunition or from storing a weapon, a particular type of weapon, or ammunition in the licensee's own motor vehicle, regardless of whether the motor vehicle is used in the course of employment or whether the motor vehicle is driven or parked on property used by the employer.

The law does not address what recourse an employer may have or what standing an employee might have should the employee constitutionally open carry a weapon. Employer prohibitions appear to only apply to "licensee" only.

Transporting

The laws regarding the transportation of handguns are found throughout Wisconsin's statutes, case law and department rules. We are going to deal with the changes in transporting handguns authorized under several WI statutes.

Transporting handguns "unloaded and encased" is still appropriate from time to time for everyone who can legally possess a handgun. For example, handguns should be transported unloaded and encased when out on the town or having a few cocktails.

When transporting a handgun it is best not to handle the handgun in any way. Every time a handgun is handled the risk of a negligent discharge goes up. For those with a carry license, getting in and out of a car, riding in a boat, riding a motorcycle, private aircraft, or an ATV do not require you to handle the weapon. The WPPA enables you to carry a loaded and uncased handgun in or on each of the above modes of transportation.

These changes in transporting a handgun also apply to those carrying constitutionally. There is a serious concern regarding how Wisconsin case law deals with "concealed handguns" when it comes to constitutional carry (a loaded and uncased handgun) in vehicles. The following case laws appear to indicate that there is no way to safely constitutionally carry a loaded and uncased handgun in a vehicle without it being considered concealed.

> In Wisconsin, a gun in plain sight inside a vehicle is both in violation of the encased requirement, Section 167.31, and considered unlawfully concealed.
>
> *State v. Walls*, 526 N.W.2d 765 (Wis. App. 1994) (A handgun on the seat of a car that was indiscernible from ordinary observation by a person outside, and within the immediate vicinity, of the vehicle was hidden from view for purposes of determining whether the

gun was a concealed weapon under this section). See also *State v. Keith*, 498 N.W.2d 865 (Ct. App. 1993) (To go armed does not require going anywhere. The elements for a violation of s. 941.23 are: 1) a dangerous weapon is on the defendant's person or within reach; 2) the defendant is aware of the weapon's presence; and 3) the weapon is hidden).

An encased gun is unlawfully concealed in a vehicle if the case is not "out of reach," arguably wingspan plus lunge distance.
State v. Alloy, 616 N.W.2d 525 (Wis. App. 2000) (affirming concealed carry conviction of man possessing handgun in a vehicle in conformity with Wisconsin Stat. 167.31 because Alloy's argument is based on the false assertion that he was trapped by a conflict between Wis. Stat. 167.31 and Wis. Stat. 941.23. A person transporting a firearm is governed by both statutes. To comply with 167.31, the person must encase the weapon. To comply with 941.23, he or she must place the enclosed weapon out of reach. See *State v. Asfoor*, 75 Wis.2d 411, 433-34, 249 N.W.2d 529 (1977). A person complying with 167.31 is not required to violate 941.23. The encased weapon can be lawfully transported out of reach.)

Locking the gun in the glove box is also still unlawful concealment.
State v. Fry, 388 N.W.2d 565 (Wis. App. 1986) (defendant was properly convicted under this section for driving a vehicle with a gun locked in a glove compartment).

Denial, suspension, revocation of license

A denial may only be issued if the applicant fails to meet one of the issuing criteria. They are as follows:

- The individual is less than 21 years of age.
- The individual is prohibited under federal law from possessing a firearm
- The individual is prohibited from possessing a firearm under Wisconsin statute (Wis. Stat. 941.29)
- The court has prohibited the individual from possessing a dangerous weapon (Wis. Stat. 969.02(3)(c) or 969.03(1)(c))

- The individual is on release and the individual may not possess a dangerous weapon as a condition of the release. (Wis. Stat. 969.01)
- The individual is not a Wisconsin resident. This means that non-resident licenses are not available.
- The individual has not provided accepted proof of training

A suspension may only occur if the court has prohibited the licensee from possessing a dangerous weapon. This may occur if the licensee is under indictment for a crime disqualifying the person from possessing a weapon. The party to the suspension or revocation will be notified by mail and will be required to deliver the license to the DOJ either personally or by certified mail.

Failure to deliver the license without an explanation is not acceptable. The licensee has seven (7) days to comply with their obligation to surrender the license.

Revocation may occur if the department determines that any of the following apply to the licensee.

- The individual is prohibited under federal law from possessing a firearm
- The individual is prohibited from possessing a firearm under Wisconsin statute (Wis. Stat. 941.29)
- The court has prohibited the individual from possessing a dangerous weapon (Wis. Stat. 969.02(3)(c) or 969.03(1)(c))
- The individual is on release and the individual may not possess a dangerous weapon as a condition of the release. (Wis. Stat. 969.01)
- The individual is not a Wisconsin resident. This means that non-resident licenses are not available.
- The individual has not provided accepted proof of training

An individual who has been denied, suspended or revoked may appeal to the Department of Justice for the decision to be reviewed. Within 30 days of receiving a notice of denial, suspension or revocation and individual may also directly petition for review to the circuit court in the county of residence without regard to any review requested from the Department of Justice.

The DOJ process should take no longer that 15 days once they have received notice of appeal.

The circuit court may take as long as it takes review the petition, the answer and any documents or records submitted by either party or the court may schedule a hearing and take testimony. In other words, the wheels of justice may turn slowly or very slowly.

The court shall reverse the department's action if any of the following are found:

- That the department failed to follow any procedure, or take any action, prescribed under this section.
- That the department erroneously interpreted a provision of law and a correct interpretation compels a different action.
- That the department's action depends on a finding of fact that is not supported by substantial evidence in the record.
- If the appeal is regarding a denial, that was based on factors other than the criteria for licensure.

If the court reverses the department's action, the court may also award court costs, and reasonable attorney's fees.

License renewal

The license is valid for five years from date of issuance (not including any military overseas deployment plus 90 days after the end of deployment). **Notice of renewal will be sent to the licensee by the department 90 days prior to expiration along with the application.**

The applicant has up to 90 days after expiration to submit the application, a statement that all the information is true and complete to the best of the applicants' knowledge that they are not disqualified from issuing criteria and appropriate fees.

The department has up to 21 days to mail a renewed license.

Crimes & related offenses

Prohibited conduct for anyone possessing a weapon includes actions and behavior for anyone (sheep, wolves and sheepdogs) and contains some pretty serious consequences. One of the reasons we can say that "an armed society is a polite society" is because of the consequences of being a "jerk with a gun" are a lot higher than just being a jerk.

The WPPA statute do not, except where noted elsewhere, change any other existing laws governing the conduct of individuals and the use of weapons. For example, the following conduct is still prohibited:

- Disorderly conduct. Where the facts and circumstances indicate a malicious or illegal intent a person may be prosecuted for loading, carrying, or going armed with a firearm. (Wis. Stat. 947.01(1) and (2)).
- Carrying a concealed firearm while intoxicated. It is a class A misdemeanor (up to 9 months jail and/or $10,000 fine) for someone to go armed while under the influence of an intoxicant. (Wis. Stat. 941.20(1)(b)). "Under the Influence" has been defined as materially impairing the ability to handle a firearm which is further explained as consuming "an amount of alcohol to cause the person to be less able to exercise clear judgment and steady hand necessary to handle a firearm." WI Jury Instruction-CRIMINAL 1321.
- Carry a firearm while unlawfully using controlled substances. It is a class A Misdemeanor (up to 9 months jail and/or $10,000 fine) to go armed with a firearm with a detectable amount of a restricted controlled substance in their blood without proof of a valid prescription. (Wis. Stat. 941.20(1)(bm)).
- Intentionally point a firearm at another unless such conduct is privileged. (Wis. Stat. 941.20(1)(c)).
- Intentionally point a firearm at a law enforcement officer, fire fighter, EMT, first responder, ambulance driver or commission warden acting in their official capacity. (Wis. Stat. 941.20(1m)).
- Intentionally discharge a firearm into a vehicle or building under circumstances in which the person should realize there might be a human being present unless privileged. (Wis. Stat. 941.20(2)).
- Intentionally discharges a firearm from a vehicle while on a highway or in a parking lot unless justified or privileged. (Wis. Stat. 941.20(3), 167.30(2));
- Possess, purchase, sell, offers to sell, manufacture, or go armed with a switchblade knife. (Wis. Stat. 941.24 (9 months jail and/or $10,000 fine)).
- Possess tear gas, mace or similar substance except for pepper spray. (Wis. Stat. § 941.26(1)(b) and (4)).

- Use tear gas or similar substances or pepper spray against a law enforcement officer or during a crime. (Wis. Stat. 941.26(2) and (4)).
- Possess, purchase, sell, transport or use a machinegun unless authorized by law. (Wis. Stat. 941.26(1m) and (3)).
- Possess, purchase, sell, transport or use a short-barreled shotgun or rifle (shotgun with a barrel length of less than 18 inches or an overall length of less than 26 inches and a rifle with a barrel length of less than 16 inches or an overall length of less than 26 inches) unless specifically allowed by the statute to possess, sell, transport or use (military in the line of duty, any peace officer of the United States or political subdivision thereof, and anyone who has complied with federal registration and licensing requirements. (Wis. Stat. 941.28).
- Sell or distribute an imitation firearm. (Wis. Stat. 941.297).
- Carry or display a facsimile firearm in a manner that could reasonably be expected to alarm, intimidate, threaten or terrify another person. (Wis. Stat. 941.2965).
- Possess, sell or deliver a firearm silencer unless specifically allowed by law. (Wis. Stat. 941.298).
- Endanger the safety of another by the negligent operation of handling of a dangerous weapon. (Wis. Stat. 941.20(1)(a) (up to 9 months jail and/or $10,000 fine).
- Recklessly endanger the safety of another person. (Wis. Stat. 941.30).
- Homicide by negligent handling of a dangerous weapon. (Wis. Stat. 940.08).
- Homicide by intoxicated use of a firearm. (Wis. Stat. 940.09).

Offenses relating to a license

DOJ is authorized to enforce the offense of false swearing with respect to false statements submitted or made in an application for a license or an application to renew a license. False swearing: (Wis. Stat. 946.32).

Firearms instructor who intentionally submit false documentation indicating that a person has met the training requirements may be prosecuted under (Wis. Stat. 946.32 (false swearing). (Wis. Stat. 175.60(17) (c)).

- Failure to provide updated address to DOJ carries a warning for a first violation (Wis. Stat. 175.60(11)(b)2). For a second violation a forfeiture of $50. (Wis. Stat. 175.60(17)(ac)).
- If the person's license is suspended or revoked and fails to submit a timely change of address individual is subject to a forfeiture of $50. (Wis. Stat. 175.60(11)(b)(3) and 175.60(17)(ac)).
- A licensee may not be charged with a violation if the department learns of the violation when the licensee informs the department of the address change (Wis. Stat. 175.60(11)(b)4)).
- Intentional failure to return a license after revocation or suspension or signed statement that the holder no longer possess the license shall be fined not more than $500 or imprisoned for not more than 30 days in jail or both. (Wis. Stat. 175.60(17)(e)).
- A person who does not carry or display a license and photo ID as required may be required to forfeit not more than $25 except that the a person is exempt from this penalty if, within 48 hours of the request, he or she presents their license document and photographic identification to the law enforcement agency that employs the law enforcement officer who lawfully requested the documents. (Wis. Stat.§ 175.60(17)(a) and (ac)).
- Carrying a concealed weapon with a license in a prohibited location may be fined not more than $500 or jailed for not more than 30 days jail or both. (Wis. Stat. 175.60(17)(c)).

A person who is issued a license and who does any of the following is guilty of a Class A misdemeanor (punishable by up to 9 months jail and/or $10,000 fine): (Wis. Stat. 946.71(2)).

- Intentionally represents as valid any revoked, suspended, fictitious, or fraudulently altered license.
- Intentionally sells or lends the license to any other individual or knowingly permits another individual to use the license.
- Intentionally represents as one's own any license not issued to him or her.
- Intentionally permits any unlawful use of that license.
- Intentionally reproduces by any means a copy of a license for a purpose that is prohibited.
- Intentionally defaces or intentionally alters a license.

- Carrying a concealed weapon without a license is a class A misdemeanor (up to 9 months jail and/or $10,000 fine). This would apply to any concealed weapon including a firearm, electric weapon, knife, billy club, etc.

Other weapons

Electronic control devices

These are electronic shock weapons. There are two varieties commonly used. The first is commonly called a "stun gun" and is a hand-held weapon that requires you to make direct contact with the attacker. The weapon will then discharge an electric current that should disrupt the attacker's ability to control their muscles.

There are a couple of disadvantages for use of a stun gun. First is the proximity issue. The victim must allow the attacker to be within an arm's length which is generally not a good idea. Since the primary purpose of a weapon is to stop the threat and create an opportunity for you to escape being closer to the attacker is counterproductive. Secondly, once the contact between the weapon and attacker breaks the affect of the current stops.

The second type of electronic control device shoots a barbed projectile connected by wire to the handheld device. Once the barbs make contact with the attacker the electrical circuit is completed and the flow of electricity disrupts the ability of the attacker to control their  muscles. The well known and largest seller of this device is made by Taser International.

This weapon is preferred by law enforcement because they can use the weapon to control a subject at a ten to fifteen foot distance and still be effective. Some models allow the user to deliver additional shocks if necessary.

The cost is one of several disadvantages for this device. The cartridges are single use and relatively expensive.

 The user is dependent on two separate operating systems. The first propels the barbs and the second delivers the shock. The barbs must make contact for current to flow and the bad guys know this. They

will pull the barbs out at their first opportunity to prevent you applying additional shocks. If one misses or does not penetrate clothing the affect is nil. The bottom line with this type of electronic control device is that you really have only one chance to create an opportunity to escape.

Both types of electronic control devices are battery dependant. This means regular maintenance whether used or not used.

The decision to carry (or use) a less than lethal weapon is a personal one. Also remember that additional unintended injury may result from the use of this weapon. The attacker may fall from a height causing serious or great bodily injury, including death. They could hit a hard surface during the fall and sustain significant injury.

The law around when the use of an electronic control device is murky at best. Since carrying an electronic control device is fairly new for citizens there is little case law to guide us. Case law for law enforcement use exists, and although generally favorable regarding its use, may not apply for citizen use.

Electronic control devices are classified in statute as a dangerous weapon. We expect the same four elements to use of lethal force must be present to justify the privilege of using an electronic control device.

These weapons were designed for use by law enforcement to gain control of a subject. An officer's handgun is almost always used for self-defense. An electronic control device is not designed for self-defense (to stop a threat).

Additionally, Wisconsin's new weapons law only allows for carrying of this type of weapon. It does not specify any specific electronic control device training or provide any legal justification when the use of electronic weapons is authorized.

There are specific places where electronic control device weapons may not be carried (for example 1-12 schools). The posting section of the WPPA appears to only applies to firearms. Be aware the some establishments may want to stretch that to include electronic control devices also. There is the risk someone may try to unlawfully (in our opinion) trespass you.

Billy club

The WPPA allows for the carrying of a "Billy Club". The billy club can be either a wood, plastic fixed-length or a metal expandable impact weapon (both types are pictured at right).

A billy club is one level up the escalation of force continuum from electronic control devices. It falls in the level of intermediate dangerous weapons. This is because it can cause a physical injury either temporary injury or permanent injury, up to death.

As with the electronic control devices you must be in close quarters to the attacker. Not quite arm's length but still uncomfortably close.

One real life example of a billy club being used against an attacker involved a bouncer who had escorted a patron out of the bar. The patron threaten the bouncer and returned to the bar with a knife intending to carry out his threat to the bouncer. The bouncer first used a billy club that failed to prevent the attacker from seriously cutting him. The bouncer then turned to his handgun and stopped the attacker. The attacker died of his injuries. The District Attorney's review of this case was simple and straightforward. Because the bouncer used an escalation of force and the less than lethal force failed to stop the attacker his use of lethal force was justified, and he was exonerated and never charged.

There are three lessons in this example. The use of the baton may have worked so it was appropriate to give it a try in this case, and there was enough time to use it. Secondly, the failure of the baton to work in stopping the attack justified the need to escalate the level of force. Third, matching or exceeding the level of force presented by the attacker is important. In this case, he bouncer tried to stop the threat with an equal or arguable slightly lesser level of force. He had the time and training to do so. In the end, the bouncer used a weapon that was one level above the attacker's weapon and successfully stopped the threat. This is an example of the old axiom, "don't bring a knife to a gun fight", or, "don't bring a billy club to a knife fight".

The Wisconsin Department of Justice outlines the techniques needed for law enforcement to use a billy club and when it is justified. Granted, law enforcement instruction is based on gaining control of a suspect or group and not necessarily self-defense. As with electronic control devices, billy clubs are not designed as a self-defense tool.

From a self-defense position the billy club is used to impede an attacker and create an opportunity to escape an attack. It is not designed to stop the threat. The Wisconsin DOJ instructions for officers has been tweaked for citizens as appropriate. These instructions are for citizens who have decided

to only carry a baton. If you are also carrying a handgun the "strong hand" and "weak hand" instructions must be reversed if you carry your handgun on your strong side.

The appropriate target areas for baton strikes are the lower abdominal area (Baton Jab), the knee and elbow area (Angle Strike and Angle-Cross Strike). The intentional use of a baton to strike the head of a subject carries with it a high propensity for serious injury or death. Therefore, although use of the baton is not classified as deadly force, an intentional strike to the head could be considered excessive force unless special circumstances justified it.

Drawing the Baton
The baton is normally carried on the strong side. If you are right handed, your strong side is your right side and vice versa.

1. Verbal warning. Deliver a verbal warning, using heavy control talk. Example: "Stop don't hurt me, Stop don't hurt me"
2. Present the baton. Place your strong hand on the baton in its holder, while moving into a defensive stance and bringing your weak hand to a high guard position. Continue with the verbal warning, escalating your verbal tone.
3. Remove the baton from the holder with your strong hand. (If using an expandable baton, expand it.). Hold the baton with both hands, strong hand near your body and weak hand near the tip, with the baton held horizontal and the tip pointing at the subject. Keep your elbows in and your stance wide and deep. Continue to issue verbal commands.
4. Load the baton. Using your strong hand, rotate the baton along a horizontal plane approximately 180º so that it remains horizontal, but now the butt is pointed toward the subject, and the tip is next to your bicep/shoulder area. Hold your weak side arm in a high guard position, with the palm facing the subject and the fingers extended as if to say "Stop!" Verbalize: "Don't hurt me!"

Baton Techniques
If drawing, presenting, and loading the baton do not cause the attacker to cease his or her behavior, the next step is to strike with the baton. There are five available options:

1. Baton Jab
2. Baton Jab – Multiple Strikes
3. Angle Strike
4. Angle-Cross Strike
5. Multiple/Overload Strikes

Baton Jab. The baton jab is effective at close quarters to move an attacker to give you time to properly load your baton. In close quarters or with an attacker, you may have to deliver a palm-heel with your strong hand to create distance and time for you to draw your baton. To apply the technique:

1. Present the baton, using your weak hand to establish a grip near the tip of the baton, and your strong hand to establish a firm grip 6" - 8" from the opposite end. The baton should be parallel to the ground.
2. Issue a loud verbal directive ("Go away!").
3. If the attacker does not retreat, thrust the end of the baton into the attacker's lower abdomen to stop his or her forward momentum and give you an opportunity to escape if possible or redeploy the baton.
4. Deliver a loud verbal stun at contact ("go away").
5. Step-slide back to a defensive stance and load the baton as described earlier, keeping your weak hand in high guard position.
6. Continue to issue verbal commands and evaluate the attacker's response to determine your next appropriate action.

Baton Jab – Multiple Strikes. In close quarters, multiple strikes may be necessary to gain enough distance to escape. Rinse, lather, repeat.

Angle Strike. The Angle Strike is delivered from the "load" position. Its purpose is to impede a attacker by striking the knee and/or elbow area. To apply the technique:

1. Starting in a defensive stance, with the baton loaded, and your reaction hand in a high guard position, issue a loud verbal command ("Leave me alone!").
2. If the attacker does not comply, direct the baton in a smooth,

angled motion toward the target area—either the elbow area or the knee area.

- Hold the baton in a grip, and keep your wrist straight and your palm up. At the moment of contact tighten your grip on the baton, using all your fingers.
- Use good body mechanics to maximize power: step into the strike, rotate your hips, and lower your center.

3. At the moment of impact, deliver a loud verbal stun ("Stop!")
4. Allow the baton to remain in contact with the attacker long enough to allow full energy transfer.
5. Return the baton to the loaded position. Continue to issue verbal commands.
6. Evaluate the attacker's response and determine your next appropriate action. Watch for an opportunity to escape.

Angle-Cross Strike. The Angle-Cross strike is used when more than one strike is necessary, and using two or more Angle Strikes (delivered from the "load" position) is impractical. For example, if your first angle strike missed its target and the baton continued in an arc toward your weak side, it would be better to deliver a Cross Strike back across your body from your weak side toward your strong side than to waste time returning to the "load" position.

Multiple/Overload Strikes. It may be necessary to deliver multiple baton strikes before the attacker complies. These can be delivered to different target areas (for example, an angle strike to the elbow, followed by an angle strike to the knee), or to the same target area, using the overload principle (for example, multiple angle strikes to the knee). The appropriate response will be dictated by your tactical evaluation and threat assessment.

Knives

The WPPA license allows for the carry of a knife as a weapon. This is an escalation of force over the billy club as seen in the example above. Significant training is needed to use a knife correctly and effectively. Because the use of a knife requires close proximity the disparity of force becomes an issue. Let's face it, a knife is less intimidating that a firearm. Maintaining control of a knife is more difficult if faced with a number of attackers. The element of surprise in the defensive use of a knife is very helpful.

Because a knife is considered a lethal weapon, the four elements must be in place before it can be used legally. Under those circumstances it certainly is less effective to stop a threat immediately than a handgun. As a self-defense tool a knife is not much better than a ball point pen which when used properly is very lethal (indeed, the pen is mightier than the sword).

Miscellaneous

Unlawful use of license

It is a class A misdemeanor to alter, deface, lend, reproduce, misrepresent as valid, sell, or knowingly allow someone else to use, a license to carry.

Emergency issuance

A person may petition the court in their county of residence for an emergency license if determined to be necessary to protect the individual from death or great bodily harm and the applicant is not otherwise ineligible for a license according to the issuing criteria.

An emergency license is valid for thirty (30) days during which time the person pursues a five year license.

If the emergency license holder is found to be ineligible for a license, the emergency license shall be voided or revoked.

Lost or destroyed licenses

Lost or destroyed licenses may be replaced by submitting a statement requesting a replacement license and any part or portion of the license if available. A replacement license will be issued within 14 days.

Record keeping

A database of licenses and license holders will be maintained by the Department of justice. Data within the database is considered private data and significant penalties apply to anyone misusing the data. Data may be made public when necessary to a prosecution.

License data is available to law enforcement agencies for the purpose of validating a license, confirming that a person is a license holder, or to investigate information submitted on a application or necessary to confirm the return of a revoked or suspended license. Data allowed to be disseminated to an officer is strictly limited.

Your status as a licensee may not be shared with the general public or persons requesting verification of a license through a law enforcement officer.

Legislative report
The DOJ is required to submit a statistical report to the legislature and the governor by March 1st of each year.

Law Enforcement Officers Safety Act (LEOSA)
Eligible retired or separated law enforcement officers are issued a certificate as evidence of passing a qualifying shooting exercise. The certificate is good for one year and is valid throughout the United States. The officer must also carry an ID card issued by their former department. This is a federal program and is governed by federal law and administered by the states.

Security guards & private detectives
Persons employed as security guards or private detectives may carry a concealed handgun if they have a Wisconsin license to carry or are a current or former law enforcement officer.

Post offices

Federal facilities are governed by the United States Code of Federal Regulations.   Entering post offices should be avoided when armed. The signs posted at post offices quote two sections of federal regulation.

1. United States Code (USC) 18 USC 930 (which deals with federal facilities in general), and
2. Code of Federal Regulations (CFR) 39 CFR 232.1 (i).

However United States Code (USC) 18 USC 930 does not apply to postal facilities because 39 USC 410 exempts Post Offices from 18 USC 930 (except for theft of mail, robbing a post office, stealing postal money orders and so forth).

39 CFR 232.1 which rises from 39 USC 410 however, does govern conduct on postal property and clearly prohibits guns while on post office property. The **underlined** sections of 39 CFR 232.1 below needs your attention. By merely entering postal property, you give up your Fourth Amendment rights against search and seizure.

(a) Applicability. This section applies to all real property under the charge and control of the Postal Service, to all tenant agencies, and to all persons entering in or on such property. This section shall be posted and kept posted at a conspicuous place on all such property. This section shall not apply to:

(i) Any portions of real property, owned or leased by the Postal Service, that are leased or subleased by the Postal Service to private tenants for their exclusive use;

(ii) With respect to sections 232.1(h)(1) and 232.1(o), sidewalks along the street frontage of postal property falling within the property lines of the Postal Service that are not physically distinguishable from adjacent municipal or other public sidewalks, and any paved areas adjacent to such sidewalks that are not physically distinguishable from such sidewalks.

(b) **Inspection, recording presence.**

(1) Purses, briefcases, and other containers brought into, while on, or being removed from the property are subject to inspection. However, items brought directly to a postal facility's customer mailing acceptance area and deposited in the mail are not subject to inspection, except as provided by section 274 of the Administrative Support Manual. A person arrested for violation of this section may be searched incident to that arrest.

(2) Vehicles and their contents brought into, while on, or being removed from restricted nonpublic areas are subject to inspection. A prominently displayed sign shall advise in advance that vehicles and their contents are subject to inspection when entering the restricted nonpublic area, while in the confines of the area, or when leaving the area. Persons entering these areas who object and refuse to consent to the inspection of the vehicle, its contents, or both, may be denied entry; after entering the area without objection, consent shall be implied. A full search of a person and any vehicle driven or occupied by the person may accompany an arrest.

(3) Except as otherwise ordered, properties must be closed to the public after normal business hours. Properties also may be closed to the public in emergency situations and at such other times as may be necessary for the orderly conduct of business. Admission to properties during periods when such properties are closed to the public may be limited to authorized individuals who may be required to sign the register and display identification

documents when requested by security force personnel or other authorized individuals.

(c) - (k) omitted (not related to firearms)

(l) Weapons and explosives. Notwithstanding the provisions of any other law, rule or regulation, no person while on postal property may carry firearms, other dangerous or deadly weapons, or explosives, either openly or concealed, or store the same on postal property, except for official purposes.

(m) – (o) omitted (not related to firearms)

(p) Penalties and other law.

(1) Alleged violations of these rules and regulations are heard, and the penalties prescribed herein are imposed, either in a Federal district court or by a Federal magistrate in accordance with applicable court rules. Questions regarding such rules should be directed to the regional counsel for the region involved.

(2) Whoever shall be found guilty of violating the rules and regulations in this section while on property under the charge and control of the Postal Service is subject to fine of not more than $50 or imprisonment of not more than 30 days, or both. Nothing contained in these rules and regulations shall be construed to abrogate any other Federal laws or regulations of any State and local laws and regulations applicable to any area in which the property is situated.

(q) Enforcement.

(1) Members of the U.S. Postal Service security force shall exercise the powers of special policemen provided by 40 U.S.C. 318 and shall be responsible for enforcing the regulations in this section in a manner that will protect Postal Service property.

(2) Local postmasters and installation heads may, pursuant to 40 U.S.C. 318b and with the approval of the chief postal inspector or his designee, enter into agreements with State and local enforcement agencies to insure that these rules and regulations are enforced in a manner that will protect Postal Service property.

(3) Postal Inspectors, Office of Inspector General Criminal Investigators, and other persons designated by the Chief Postal Inspector may likewise enforce regulations in this section.

[37 FR 24346, Nov. 16, 1972, as amended at 38 FR 27824, Oct. 9, 1973; 41 FR 23955, June 14, 1976; 42 FR 17443, Apr. 1, 1977; 43

> *FR 38825, Aug. 31, 1978; 46 FR 898, Jan. 5, 1981. Redesignated and amended at 46 FR 34330, July 1, 1981; 47 FR 32113, July 26, 1982; 53 FR 29460, Aug. 5, 1988; 54 FR 20527, May 12, 1989; 57 FR 36903, Aug. 17, 1993; 57 FR 38443, Aug. 25, 1992; 63 FR 34600, June 25, 1998; 70 FR 72078, Dec. 1, 2005]*

Prosecutors like to add on other charges such as disorderly conduct and disturbing the peace for example, just to up the ante of charges against you so be mindful of the consequences.

This is a long way to say it, but if armed stay off postal property. Park your vehicle on the street or another area that is not controlled by the post office. Disarm and store your firearm in your vehicle before leaving your vehicle and enter a post office.

Of course, this advice is subject to change pending the outcome of Bonidy et al v. United States Postal Service et al, and any new federal regulations that ruling may prompt.

Non-postal Federal facilities

So, for non-postal facilities, Title 18, United States Code, Sec. 930.— Possession of firearms and dangerous weapons in federal facilities applies and is very clear (the emphasis is added):

Sec. 930. Possession of firearms and dangerous weapons in Federal facilities.

(a) Except as provided in subsection (d), whoever knowingly possesses or causes to be present a firearm or other dangerous weapon in a Federal facility (other than a Federal court facility), or attempts to do so, shall be fined under this title or imprisoned not more than 1 year, or both.

(b) Whoever, with intent that a firearm or other dangerous weapon be used in the commission of a crime, knowingly possesses or causes to be present such firearm or dangerous weapon in a Federal facility, or attempts to do so, shall be fined under this title or imprisoned not more than 5 years, or both.

(c) A person who kills any person in the course of a violation of subsection (a) or (b), or in the course of an attack on a Federal facility involving the use of a firearm or other dangerous weapon, or attempts or conspires to do such an act, shall be punished as provided in sections 1111, 1112, 1113, and 1117.

(d) Subsection (a) shall not apply to:

(1) the lawful performance of official duties by an officer, agent,

or employee of the United States, a State, or a political subdivision thereof, who is authorized by law to engage in or supervise the prevention, detection, investigation, or prosecution of any violation of law;

(2) the possession of a firearm or other dangerous weapon by a Federal official or a member of the Armed Forces if such possession is authorized by law; or

(3) the lawful carrying of firearms or other dangerous weapons in a Federal facility incident to hunting or other lawful purposes.

(e) (1) Except as provided in paragraph (2), whoever knowingly possesses or causes to be present a firearm in a Federal court facility, or attempts to do so, shall be fined under this title, imprisoned not more than 2 years, or both.

(2) Paragraph (1) shall not apply to conduct which is described in paragraph (1) or (2) of subsection (d).

(f) Nothing in this section limits the power of a court of the United States to punish for contempt or to promulgate rules or orders regulating, restricting, or prohibiting the possession of weapons within any building housing such court or any of its proceedings, or upon any grounds appurtenant to such building.

(g) As used in this section:

(1) The term "Federal facility" means a building or part thereof owned or leased by the Federal Government, where Federal employees are regularly present for the purpose of performing their official duties.

(2) The term "dangerous weapon" means a weapon, device, instrument, material, or substance, animate or inanimate, that is used for, or is readily capable of, causing death or serious bodily injury, except that such term does not include a pocket knife with a blade of less than 2 ½ inches in length.

(3) The term "Federal court facility" means the courtroom, judges' chambers, witness rooms, jury deliberation rooms, attorney conference rooms, prisoner holding cells, offices of the court clerks, the United States attorney, and the United States marshal, probation and parole offices, and adjoining corridors of any court of the United States.

(h) Notice of the provisions of subsections (a) and (b) shall be posted conspicuously at each public entrance to each Federal facility, and notice of subsection (e) shall be posted conspicuously at each public entrance to each Federal court facility, and no person shall be convicted of an offense under subsection (a) or (e) with respect to a Federal facility if such notice is not so posted at such facility, unless such person had actual notice of subsection (a) or (e), as the case may be.

Many people have seized upon (d)(3) to justify carrying a gun in a federal facility, by using the argument that they have a license to carry and their carrying of a firearm is an "other lawful purpose" so they are exempt from the prohibition.

The problem with relying on 18 USC 930(d)(3) is that this section in no way empowers anyone to carry a gun in a federal facility; rather, that section simply states that 18 USC 930 does not apply to someone lawfully carrying a gun incident to some lawful purpose. Unless specifically prohibited by Wisconsin statutes, the state generally leaves the regulation of federal property to others. The MPPA does not specifically authorize the lawful carry into a federal facility either.

It is never lawful to carry into a federal court facility; that is illegal except for law enforcement officers and certain members of military while on active duty.

But does Title 18, Section 930 mean that it is legal to carry into, say, a federal office building? That is what the exemption in the law seems to say for somebody with a license to carry and being in the building for "other lawful purposes".

Because it is a gray area, we advise you to stay out of gray areas. Test court cases are expensive and the outcome is never certain. If you wish to make this your fight, start by contacting your members of Congress to change the law.

Traveling outside of Wisconsin

If you happen to be one of those people who has lived your life close to home, you will be surprised should you decide to take a trip around the country. Besides sightseeing new terrain you will find that some states treat armed citizens very well, but you may also be surprised to find other states or cities are not so friendly.

The authority to manage the lawful carry of firearms is the responsibility reserved to each state and there is little consistency in the carry laws from one state to another. There is no (thankfully) Federal regulation governing license holders. If there ever was a Federal law that set uniform standards all across state lines you might think that would make life better. However, the trade-off for consistent carry laws is the risk of unnecessary federal conditions placed on every armed citizen or an anti-rights President overturning the rights of millions of people across the entire country. We prefer to deal with differences in laws from state to state than to hand the federal government overwhelming power over an individual's right to maintain their constant state of peace.

Whether or not another state honors a Wisconsin carry license is entirely up to the that state's legislature or perhaps a bureaucrat of that state. If the law passed by the legislature states they will recognize all other states licenses, the legislature has made the decision. On the other hand, if the legislature has authorized the state's Attorney General or another person, to determine based upon a set of criteria, which states licenses they will honor, a bureaucrat may interpret those instructions from the legislature narrowly or broadly, depending upon their personal political beliefs.

Wisconsin carry law is similar to other states in many ways but there are also some differences. The laws are subject to change at any time by the legislatures, and you should learn about the current law in a given state before carrying a gun there. For example, some states forbid carry in bars, Wisconsin allows it. Most states require that license holders carry concealed, Wisconsin allows license holders to carry openly or concealed, and in some states there are serious penalties for even accidentally displaying or showing the outline of a firearm.

Generally speaking, it is lawful to travel with an unloaded gun, ammunition stored separately, locked in a case in the trunk or the rearmost area of a vehicle, if one is simply traveling through a state, rather than staying overnight or longer. The McClure-Volkmer act also known as the Firearm Owners Act of 1986 (FOPA). deals with this. Title 18 United States Code section 926A provides:

"Notwithstanding any other provision of any law or any rule or regulation of a State or any political subdivision thereof, any person who is not otherwise prohibited by this chapter from transporting, shipping, or receiving a firearm shall be entitled to transport a firearm for any lawful purpose from any place where he may lawfully possess and carry such firearm to any other place where he may lawfully possess and carry such firearm if, during such transportation the firearm is unloaded, and neither the firearm nor any ammunition being transported is readily accessible or is directly accessible from the passenger compartment of such transporting vehicle: Provided, That in the case of a vehicle without a compartment separate from the driver's compartment the firearm or ammunition shall be contained in a locked container other than the glove compartment or console."

The protection afforded under federal law while traveling will not be helpful should you stop traveling and stay overnight. It is not legal to possess a handgun even if it is unloaded and locked in a case in the trunk of a car, while remaining in certain places such as New York City or the District of Columbia. The same principles that apply to entering the security zone of the airport apply in these places. Forgetting that you have a gun with you does not constitute an excuse should you decide to stay overnight.

The best practice is to know if you will be entering places on your trip that you need to be concerned about before you leave home. If you want to travel with your firearm consult the Attorney General's offices of the states and ask about the metropolitan areas through which you will be traveling or be staying overnight. A good resource is the website www.handgunlaw.us for reliable information about carry and who to call to get your questions answered in the fifty states.

The National Rifle Association also publishes a guide on the interstate transportation of firearms which is available from http://www.nraila.org/gun-laws/articles/2010/guide-to-the-interstate-transportation.aspx

Traveling outside the United States

When traveling outside of the United States by air, you need to be aware of the laws of your destination. Just because you may be able to get a firearm on board an airplane while in the United States, how are you going to deal with it when you arrive in another country? Is any license or permit necessary for you to possess a firearm in another country and if so, can you get one or do you have one? Have you considered if you will be allowed to return to the United States with a firearm aboard a foreign airline? What about stops and layovers during the trip? Can you travel with your favorite hollow point ammunition or are there any ammunition restrictions? Are certain types of firearms restricted or prohibited? Do you have the needed paperwork to prove you possessed the firearm and ammunition in the United States before you left home.

If traveling by land, Mexico for example is easy, the country severely restricts the importation of firearms and ammunition. Leave your firearms and ammunition at home. An exception is possible if you are bringing a firearm into Mexico for hunting purposes accompanied by a Mexican hunting guide, but you should contact your Mexican outfitter for help and information on import requirements.

Canada forbids US citizens from entering the country with handguns. Canadian Customs will permit a visitor to Canada to declare and check in guns at the border, and then retrieve them when returning to the United States. The guns should be unloaded, in a locked case, and the ammunition should be stored separately.

Canadian law prohibits the possession of hollowpoint ammunition, and if that is what you have brought with you it is important check in your ammunition as well.

The Canadian Customs station will hold the guns for up to forty days. Upon leaving Canada, you just stop at the same Customs station and produce your photo ID and the receipt. They will give the guns back to you.

You should then keep the guns cased and unloaded while proceeding down the road to US Customs. Importation of firearms or ammunition into the United States requires a permit from the Bureau of Alcohol, Tobacco, Firearms and Explosives unless the traveler can demonstrate that the firearms or ammunition were previously possessed in the United States. One way to do this is by completing Customs and Border Protection (CBP) Form 4457 with your local CBP office before leaving the United States. A bill of sale or receipt showing transfer of the items to the traveler in the United States may also be used.

In the United States you have constitutional protections both against unreasonable searches and seizures and against compelled self-incrimination. Although the authorities may search anywhere within your reach without a search warrant after a valid stop, they may not open and search closed luggage without probable cause to believe evidence of a crime will be found, particularly when it is in a locked storage area or trunk of a vehicle, unless you consent. You have a right not to consent. Furthermore, although you may be required to identify yourself and produce a driver's license, vehicle registration, and proof of automobile insurance, you have a right to remain silent.

Know the local laws of your destination.

The most important rule is to be sure, in advance, that you can lawfully possess the firearm at your destination. Specifically, know whether the specific firearm, magazines and ammunition may be lawfully possessed. State legislatures have been known to change firearms possession laws at the whim and fancy of whatever the current political reason de jour happens to be. Check early and often for any changes in the law at your destination.

Know the local laws of your destination

Know that you can lawfully possess the gun at your destination before leaving home or your point of departure. Again, the Attorney General's office of the state you are visiting or www.handgunlaw.us are good places to start.

Even if the state does not recognize Wisconsin carry licenses or one of your non-resident carry licenses, you may be legally able to keep a firearm in your hotel room. Just know what the laws are in advance.

Airports

There is no "official" count, however we believe there are somewhere around 25,000,000 armed citizens in the United States. Many of these people travel by air. Airports and airlines have met enough people who travel with a firearm, that it is no longer an "event" at the airport.

If you are just dropping off someone at the airport, there is nothing you need to do unless you plan to go into a secured area of the airport. The same is true if you are meeting someone who has arrived and you are picking them up. The baggage claim area is in an unsecured area of the airport, so you can park, go in and help carry their luggage if necessary.

If you are the traveler, things change a lot. From the TSA website:

Travelers may only transport UNLOADED firearms in a locked, hard-sided container in or as checked baggage. All firearms, ammunition and firearm parts, including firearm frames and receivers, are prohibited in carry-on baggage.

To avoid issues that could impact your travel and/or result in law enforcement action, here are regulations to assist you in packing your firearms and ammunition:

- All firearms must be declared to the airline during the ticket counter check-in process.
- The firearm must be unloaded.
- The firearm must be in a hard-sided container that is locked. A locked container is defined as one that completely secures the firearm from being accessed. Locked cases that can be pulled open with little effort cannot be brought aboard the aircraft.
- If firearms are not properly declared or packaged, TSA will provide the bag to law enforcement for resolution with the airline. If the

issue is resolved, law enforcement will release the bag to TSA so screening may be completed.

- TSA must resolve all alarms in checked baggage. If a locked container containing a firearm alarms, TSA will contact the airline, who will make a reasonable attempt to contact the owner and advise the passenger to go to the screening location. If contact is not made, the container will not be placed on the aircraft.
- If a locked container alarms during screening and is not marked as containing a declared firearm, TSA will cut the lock in order to resolve the alarm.
- Travelers should remain in the area designated by the aircraft operator or TSA representative to take the key back after the container is cleared for transportation.
- Travelers must securely pack any ammunition in fiber (such as cardboard), wood or metal boxes or other packaging specifically designed to carry small amounts of ammunition.
- Firearm magazines and ammunition magazines must be securely boxed or included within a hard-sided case containing an unloaded firearm.
- Small arms ammunition, including ammunition not exceeding .75 caliber for a rifle or pistol and shotgun shells of any gauge, may be carried in the same hard-sided case as the firearm, as long as it follows the packing guidelines described above.
- TSA prohibits black powder or percussion caps used with black-powder.
- Rifle scopes are not prohibited in carry-on bags and do not need to be in the hard-sided, locked checked bag.

Unless you are a frequent flyer and already know each airlines rules, we suggest that you ask if firearms are permitted on the airline(s) you will be flying before you purchase your ticket. Also ask about any limitations on transportation of ammunition you want to take along on your trip. Are there any other limitations you should be aware? Airlines are charging for everything these days, so ask if there is any additional charge for you to fly with a firearm.

You need to first declare the firearm when at the ticket counter and it has to be unloaded and locked in a hard or metal gun container inside of your checked luggage. Since your firearm, spare magazines, speed loaders, and ammunition are locked in your checked baggage, you might as well put your holster in your baggage too. Keeping a holster on your body will only cause you problems with hypersensitive TSA agents.

You can never ever walk through a security checkpoint while you are in possession of a gun. It does not matter if it is unloaded and secured in a locked box. This also applies to spare magazines, speed loaders, and ammunition, as well.

You should make it a habit to check all your pockets and bags before leaving for the airport so you are ready when you arrive to check your bags and go through security. You can avoid missing a flight because

you forgot that you had locked your gun in your briefcase, or need to figure out what to do with a spare magazine or speed loader. Taking the time to check to be sure your firearm and accessories were properly stored, is a small inconvenience when compared to being arrested. Besides civil fines, security violations may also lead to felony criminal charges in federal court.

You also need to know how you will handle layovers, particularly if you will be changing airlines or staying overnight. It is best if the airlines can move your checked luggage to your next flight without the need for you to take possession of it. If you must take possession and leave the airport and go to a hotel for the night, avoiding trouble in places that severely restrict the possession of firearms like New York can be very difficult. It is best that the airline retain possession of your checked luggage. Your carry on luggage should contain what you need for an overnight stay whether planned or not.

And remember: a gun never solves problems.

CHAPTER 9
The Mechanics of Everyday Carry

This chapter is about societal considerations, a contract with society as to what is acceptable and tolerable. This is an exercise in merging the rights to carry a firearm for personnel protection with the communities' right to not be scared at the sight of an armed citizen. As armed citizens, we must extend every courtesy and kindness to our fellow community members. This behavior will help the community accept armed citizens. An old Western saying captures this sentiment, "Do not scare the woman or the horses."

This chapter is also about the practical aspects of carrying a firearm.

When should I carry?

You have to make your own decisions about when to carry. A carry license gives you the right to carry a pistol, but it does not create an obligation to do so. Some license holders will carry a handgun rarely, if ever. Other will choose to carry whenever their pants are on.

Carrying only when you feel that you are in danger is an emotional way of making this decision. It is also impossible to do. By the time you realize you are in danger it is too late to go home and get your gun! If you are going to go to a dangerous area today, having rusty skills by not having carried regularly is just as dangerous. Look, random acts of violence is just that, random. To be prepared for a random attack takes regular practice. For an armed citizen this means carrying your handgun regularly and going to the range to keep your shooting skill sharp, and constantly practicing your situational awareness.

It is time to eat your own cooking. If you have decided that maintaining your constant state of peace is important to you, then you owe it to yourself, your family, friends, coworkers, anyone who appreciates you to support that decision.

Maintaining your *constant* state of peace means; *carry all the time* and be prepared to store the gun when necessary.

Choosing a carry method or, a combination of carry methods, that will work for you in each of the seasons, requires a little planning.

Pistol petting

"Pistol petting" refers to the tendency of someone who is new to carrying to be constantly checking the holster to make sure the gun is still there. Do not do this. The women and horses may be watching.

Avoid accidental exposure

A gun in a hip holster may be exposed if, for example, you sweep your jacket back to retrieve your wallet. It is much better to reach back, behind and underneath the hem of the jacket, and retrieve the wallet without exposing the handgun. This feels strange at first, but with a little practice it becomes natural. Most armed citizens get into the habit of carrying their wallet on the opposite side of their body where they carry their handgun.

Your concealed handgun may become unconcealed or noticeable under your cover garment. The latter is called "printing". This is when the outline of the handgun can be unintentionally detected through a cover garment. As Wisconsinites become more comfortable with the sight of armed citizens this will not be a big deal. You are behaving as a sheepdog so there is nothing wrong or illegal if people see your gun as long as you are not threatening them.

If it is necessary to adjust your firearm, discretion is good. Should you desire to move the gun from a hip holster to a coat pocket holster, practice at home might be good. Move the firearm as if it were a wallet or checkbook, easy and without any excess movement. Practice will make this appear as nothing of interest is happening.

The belt

One aspect about carrying on a hip holster is the fact that *the belt itself is just as important as the holster*. Thin, flexible belts are perfectly adequate to keep a pair of pants from falling down, but they are not rigid enough to keep a holster with a handgun weighing a pound or more in a stable position.

Most commercial leather belts 1.5 to 1.75 inch wide do not have the required stiffness to firmly control the holster. We recommend purchasing one or more belts that have been specially designed for use with a holster. Some of these are leather belts with *polymer* inserts through ¾ of their length, some are double thick all leather. A good carry belt prevents both twist and sag of the handgun.

Carry methods

There are several different basic carry methods and an almost unlimited number of combinations. They can be reduced to the following categories: hip holster, shoulder holster, pocket holster, deep cover carry, off-body carry, and a few alternative methods, each with their own advantages and disadvantages.

Because of both physical and social differences between men and women, the subject of carry for women has some special issues, and we will cover that in its own section.

Holsters

The most common way to carry a handgun is in a holster. All good holsters have two important characteristics in common; (1) they must cover the trigger guard completely, and (2) they must support the gun in precisely the same position each time, without letting it flop around.

This is why a holster must always be used. *Never, never carry a handgun without a proper holster*. An unholstered handgun will result, sooner or later, in a negligent discharge and significant injury *to you*. You have been warned.

Hip holsters

Hip holster are the most common carry method that combines both security and accessibility. The hip holster holds the gun on the on the hip outside of the pant waist on a belt. Hip holsters are typically worn on the "strongside" hip (the right hip for right-handers; the left hip for

lefties), at or behind the hip joint. There are also cross draw, center of back, and inside the waistband belt holsters.

To conceal carry requires wearing a covering garment over the handgun, a coat, jacket, vest or a loose shirt. Some hip holsters allow a shirt to be tucked in around them but there still may be noticeable printing. Printing may also occur with an untucked shirt or blouse.

As long as you are wearing a covering garment that can be quickly brushed aside, this keeps the gun reasonably available and well-concealed. During winter months a gun on a belt holster under two sweaters and a zipped-up parka will be anything but quickly available. A pocket holster in the parka will solve this problem.

There are all sorts of hip holsters. The one on the right has a retaining device called a "thumb break". A thumb break holster is in the category of a level one holster because there is one "retention" feature. This is a minimum for open carry and is highly advised for concealed carry.

Holsters vary dramatically both in configuration and quality. We recommend trying a number of different ones. Holsters are like clothing. There are a lot of manufacturers and no one

store carries them all. When shopping for your carry gun, check out the holsters manufactured for that specific model. Remember the more exotic the handgun the fewer the holster options. New models may also have a smaller selection. An online search is a good place to start the holster shopping process.

Your handgun is a "working gun" and your holster should also be a "working holster". Consider how the holster will treat the gun. A padded nylon holster or a mid-range to high-end leather will be gentle on the handgun, a polymer holster, not so much. The thickness and quality of the leather gives an indication of how long this holster may serve you or how well it functions.

Cost alone is not necessarily an indicator of a good or bad holster. An inexpensive holster can still be a good holster, fit well and securely hold

the handgun. An expensive black leather holster may be just right for a night out on the town, a wedding or a formal charity affair.

Custom made holsters may seem pretentious, but are an affordable way to solve problems not resolved by mass market holsters. Leather shops know they can custom build a holster to fit you and your budget. Can you spend $300? Sure. But you can also spend only $50.

Inside the waistband

One very good type of hip holster, is an "inside the waistband," or IWB, holster. Instead of wearing the holster on the outside of the pant, this holster is slipped inside the waistband of the pants and is secured to the belt to keep it from falling down the inside of your pant. The example at right shows two "clips" that go over the top of the waistband and the belt. The belt also presses the holster and handgun into place.

Some IBW holsters allow for the shirt to be "tucked" in between the holster and the waistband giving the appearance of an ordinary tucked in shirt trouser combination. For many people this is an advantage. The entire handgun is concealed with a very conventional style of dress. Only a strap is visible on the belt.

Unless you already have pants that fit loosely around the waist, you will have to buy new trousers with an additional inch or two in the waistband. Some people, especially those with bad backs, find that the pressure against the side and back can become painful. High-tech plastics such as Kydex can be perfectly fine for a traditional hip holster on the belt, however the stiffness of the plastic tends to make them uncomfortable when they are pushed up strongly against the body.

Some IWB holsters are soft-sided, and the mouth of the holster will collapse when the gun is removed, making re-holstering a complicated, two-hand operation sometimes requiring undoing the belt. This is not particularly a problem for somebody who is keeping his gun on his hip all day, but presents ongoing difficulties for people who constitutionally carry and have to store the handgun to comply with statutes regarding being within 1000 feet of a school.

Shoulder holsters

Cover garments are strongly recommended for this type of holster. The covering garment has to cover the gun and all of the straps.

Shoulder holsters come in two varieties, a vertical or horizontal holster position. A vertical holster has the barrel pointing down and the back of the grip is near your armpit. The horizontal holster has the barrel of the gun pointing at everyone behind you and the top of slide or barrel is near your armpit. Safety conscious armed citizens do not take kindly to  the horizontal shoulder holster because it is pointing the gun in an unsafe direction even when it is in the holster.

 Shoulder holsters can be uncomfortable. The straps tend to cut into the shoulders. Both the strong (holster) side and the weak side need to secure the holster. They are not designed to be suspenders so must be secured to a belt. Shoulder holsters do not

offer much "give" as the wearer moves around. This can cause cervical neck and back pain.

Shoulder holsters and holster worn cross draw have a common problem. When drawing your handgun, if bystanders are present, there is a high probability to sweep (momentarily point) the gun at persons other than your target. As the handgun comes out of the holster, the barrel becomes parallel with the ground and rotated towards the target and the muzzle crosses anyone who is standing in the way.

Our recommendation is that shoulder holsters be thought of as special-purpose holsters and not be a prime candidate for day-to-day carry.

Pocket holsters

Pocket holsters are a terrific choice for many people, particularly those carrying smaller guns, a backup gun, or for woman. Anything other than overly tight pants makes them very concealable, and the ability to reach into a pocket without doing anything dramatic enable you to get a grip on the handgun without having to commit yourself to displaying it.

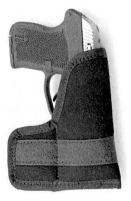

The primary purpose of the pocket holster is to protect the trigger by covering the trigger guard. A handgun should never be carried loose in a pocket unless you want to shoot yourself. Of course that leads to a whole new set of problems!

Pocket holsters have the advantage of being able to fit into different kinds of pockets. The same holster can work in the pant pocket, a coat pocket, or even in the chest pocket of a parka.

The pocket holds the gun in position. A good pocket holster will have one of a number of different ways of keeping the holster in the pocket when drawing the handgun.

A few pocket holsters are designed with a leather square stitched to the outside of the holster that gives it the outline of a wallet even in a tight pants pocket. This allows the handgun to be carried in a back pocket if desired.

For those interested in pocket carry, we recommend a combination of a small hammerless revolver and a rigid pocket holster as a good starting point. Many experienced armed citizens find pocket carry is a satisfactory backup carry method, or a great way to carry when any inadvertent exposure from a hip holster will not do.

An advantage of pocket carry is that it enables you in a stressful situation to get your handgun *in your hand* without committing yourself to drawing it or displaying it. Instead of sweeping back your jacket as you would have to with a belt holster or shoving your hand under your jacket as you would need to with a shoulder holster, all you have to do is insert your hand in your pocket. That is something people do all the time and it does not draw attention to you.

Deep cover

Beyond standard holsters there is a whole variety of "deep cover" alternatives. Deep cover holsters are those that allow the handgun to be completely hidden with no printing.

One common type of holster in this category is what is called the "belly band." This is basically a broad elastic bandage with an attached holster, and it is worn under the shirt or blouse. It does conceal very well but it is necessary to either unbutton the shirt or yank it up in order to get at the gun. It works best for people with flat stomachs.

Kramer Leather makes what they call their "Confidant Shirt Holster." Basically, it is an armless t-shirt with a built-in elastic holster under each armpit. It is worn much as a t-shirt is under any shirt or other clothing and just as is true for the belly band, it can make retrieving a gun very difficult, but it conceals very well. The only additional disadvantage is that the t-shirt

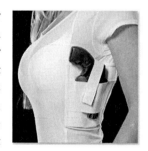

itself is, for structural reasons, made from polypropylene rather than cotton and can be uncomfortable, particularly when worn for extended periods of time.

Perhaps the strangest, no it is the strangest "deep cover" carry method is the under-the-pants pouch sold by the brand names of Thunderwear™

 or Thunderbelt™. The gun is carried in a breathable plastic or denim pouch on the front of the waist just over the crotch, or slightly to the side with the butt either below the belt or the belt resting on the butt of the gun with the barrel pointing in a very unsafe direction.

The real problem with Thunderwear and similar holsters is your safety. Either holstering or retrieving the gun requires pointing it at your crotch, and that violates the safety principle of "never point a gun at anything you are not willing to destroy." Use this form of carry *at your own risk!*

Alternative carry methods

Those that feel it is important to carry more than one handgun need a suitable back-up carry method. Something other than the double six-shooter holsters of Roy Rogers, an early back-up gun carry method.

Ankle holster

An ankle holster is a good choice. At first glance, it does have some advantages. For example, the trouser leg covers the pistol. Considering that many random acts of violence have the attacker immediately on top of the victim, or the victim pushed to the ground getting to an ankle holster may actually be easier than getting to a hip holster.

It has been said that the ankle holster puts the gun as far away from the hand as it can be and still be on the body while you are standing. While true, the ankle is not where you carry your primary handgun. So the distance to reach your ankle holstered back-up gun rarely is an issue.

Fanny packs

Also in the alternative carry category are the various "fanny packs" specifically designed to carry a handgun. There is a concealed compartment, closed either by a zipper or Velcro fastenings, which importantly keeps the gun separate from other items being carried. The gun is reasonably accessible and the fanny pack is also useful for keys, wallets, change and cell phones. Major holster manufacturers make some form of fanny pack holster.

Fanny packs are definitely handy but they are not for everybody or every situation. They look distinctly out of place in most office or more formal settings. The general rule for using a fanny pack to carry a handgun is that it should be used in situations where fanny packs are already commonly worn. You will find them in abundance at the malls, or on people taking walks in parks and so forth. Fanny packs are great for woman.

The main problem with fanny packs used for handguns is what to do when you take them off? As a matter of safety and common sense either the gun or the fanny pack containing the gun must be securely stored when it is not on the body.

Small of the back holsters

One convenient carry method idea is the small-of-the-back (SOB) holster. Instead of being worn on or just behind the hip the holster, usually with a dramatic cant, goes on the belt in the middle of the back.

There is just one advantage to this mode of carry. There is little danger of a covering garment being inadvertently swept so far aside that the firearm is revealed.

The main problem with small of the back carry is safety. The holster positions the handgun out of your sight but makes maintaining control of the handgun difficult at best. If the gun is discovered, it can be taken away from you before you can react. If under an attack, there is a question how fast and troublesome your handgun can be deployed and that you are going to sweep yourself in the process.

This form of carry requires at least a level one retention holster and a level two would be better. You will need to be able to quickly manipulate the holsters safety devices without the benefit of sight which may seriously slow you down.

Putting a piece of hard metal up against your spine is not a very good idea. When sitting, the handgun is uncomfortably pressed against your lower back. A fall onto the back from an attack is more likely to cause spinal injury with a small of the back.

Cross draw

Another option is the cross-draw holster. Instead of being on or behind the strong-side hip the holster sits on the weak-side of the belt, with the butt of the grip canted forward. Cross draw holsters allow the armed citizen a faster draw. Because it takes less time to deploy your handgun, you have more time to assess the situation, decide on a plan and take action.

Cross draw holsters have an advantage for those who spend most of their time sitting while carrying, such as truck drivers or anyone confined to a wheel chair.

Cross draw carry is for an average proportioned person. For those people who enjoy a bit more girth, cross draw maybe physically difficult and can be uncomfortable.

Off-body carry

There is not much good we can say about off-body carry. It is important that when you are carrying a handgun in public *it be under your direct personal control at all times,* and that is difficult to do unless it is on your body.

For example, some manufacturers make purses, daily planners and briefcases with hidden compartments. A photographer's bag can easily conceal a handgun in one of its compartments.

None of these choices should be used. An attacker recognizes a purse, day planner or briefcase as a target of opportunity. It certainly is if your handgun is inside.

The problem with any form of off-body carry is that, in an emergency situation, the armed citizen is physically separated your their handgun. The only good place for a self-defense handgun is on your body.

The bathroom

Those who are new to carrying a handgun in public will have to learn how to deal with using a public rest room. In the case of a single-user rest room with a lock on the door there is no problem. You simply use the facility readjust your clothing, holster and handgun and leave. If you remove the handgun from the holster for some reason, do not forget it. There are numerous reports of armed citizens and law enforcement officers forgetting their handguns in the bathroom only to return and find them gone.

Typical public bathrooms do not provide that level of privacy. What is important to avoid is to have a person in the next stall seeing the holstered handgun lying on the floor. It is fair to say that the other patrons of the bath room are not expecting to see a handgun lying on the floor holstered or not. You have no idea who may be in the next stall and a gun on the floor is an attractive theft opportunity. Needless to say, you are not in a position to give chase either.

Handling or fondling the handgun while on the throne has resulted in serious thigh burns and significant repair to the facility. *Do not* play with the handgun. The poor person in the next stall does not deserve to get shot no matter odorous their business.

The successful use of a public restroom stall is to keep the handgun out of sight and under your control. This may mean laying the handgun in the cradle of your slacks. Putting the handgun in a jacket pocket will also work. Develop a personal approach that is safe, discrete and allows you to maintain control of the handgun and use it consistently. Never hang the handgun on the coat hook on the back of the door.

Depending on how you carry your handgun, using a urinal may pose an issue. It may just be better to use a stall. Otherwise, the configuration of the rest room may allow you to use a urinal next to a wall that will provide protection for your handgun.

Carrying for women

Women have special issues when it comes to carrying self defense handguns for cultural, physiological and physical reasons. Rather than attempt to discuss this as though we knew first hand all about a woman's needs, we will demonstrate through pictures, some of the creative ways a woman could carry.

A woman should choose her own carry gun not only because she needs it to fit her hand, but because of the style of carry she may want to use.

As a historical matter, most belt holsters were designed for men. Because of generally different shapes in the hip area, and where the waist of women's slacks or skirts are relative to men's, a handgun carried in a typical belt holster will leave the muzzle pushed out by the swell of a woman's hip. This also tilts the gun so that the butt digs into a woman's side and can be uncomfortable.

For police service holsters for women this problem has been solved by adding spacers, which hold the top of the holster further out from

Behind the back   Compact belt hip   Inside the waist band

the hip. That is a fine solution for uniformed women police officers but does not help women who want to carry concealed. The butt of the pistol sticks out significantly, and that is the sort of bulge that will be noticed under any covering garment. For women carrying openly spacers will work fine. For women while wearing jeans or slacks and a jacket or vest, a belt and holster combination is every bit as practical as it is for men.

We still need to address the question about how to carry a concealed handgun when wearing a dress or a skirt and blouse. In both cases, the typical belts are usually rather thin, and a covering garment of some sort is usually worn. Similarly, for those women who wear suited skirts and similar attire, the matter of the where to put a holster can be handled by proper selection. In this case wearing a holster on a belt may not be the best option.

Shoulder holsters or a concealment shirt with a holster built under the arm are a practical solution when worn under a covering garment. Women's arms are longer in relation to the width of their shoulders, so it is usually easy for a woman to reach across the chest and grip a pistol in a shoulder holster.

Some limitations apply because these types of holsters must be covered by some garment. Women who wear sufficiently loose blouses or shirts, could wear a holster under their blouse or shirt.

Womens underwear can also multi-task for those who carry a handgun. If you are wearing underwear anyway, why not make more use of it?

For those times when it is just easier to put one somewhere else on your body we can offer several good choices to consider.

LEOSA Trainers, Inc.

One place many women consider to carry a handgun is in a purse or the equivalent, and some manufacturers do make purses with concealed pockets specifically for handguns. We recommend against this type of carry for many good reasons. Even the most situationally alert people occasionally lapse in attention for just a moment, and if your purse is snatched, you will also lose control over your handgun to a criminal. If you are attacked, it is much more difficult and time consuming to locate and use a handgun if it is stored away in a purse. During the day at work, it will be necessary to lock the entire purse in a desk drawer, leaving it available to anybody who has the key to the desk and inaccessible to you should you need your handgun quickly. Any time a purse is resting on a counter, a shopping cart, or anywhere it is away from you, you have violated the contract with society to maintain immediate control over your handgun.

We strongly recommend on body carry for women. As the photos illustrate, there are many different options available to work with most any wardrobe.

Storing when carrying

There are often times when it may be necessary to store a gun while away from home: you may need to enter a prohibited place like a post office or school, you may not be able to carry at work, you may decide to go out for a few beers with a friend, or any of a myriad of other things.

When you do that the gun must be securely stored and it is important to decide how to do that in advance.

We recommend securing the gun in a lockable container inside a locked car. If your evening out includes drinking alcohol and you cannot go home to store your gun first, we recommend unloading the gun before locking it up and do not touch it again until you are completely sober.

It is equally important to keep the gun from being stolen. We have an implied contract with society to maintain control of our handguns. It is a good idea to do the same with any weapon you are authorized to carry. Simply leaving a weapon in a car is a bad idea. All cars can be broken into in a matter of seconds by thieves in a number of ways. Gloves boxes will not stop anyone. The plastic latches on most cars' glove compartments are remarkably weak. Other "hiding" places in a vehicle are poor substitutes

for investing in the right storage equipment.

The Secure-It is designed to reduce the possibility of theft of a handgun from a vehicle. The lockable metal box is small enough to be hidden under the seat, and it comes with a strong steel cable that tethers the box to a seat support or other permanent structure of the vehicle. The Secure-It lends itself to discreetly storing the handgun. From the outside it looks as if you are just taking a moment to complete a phone call or gather some items. Deterring a thief just four minutes can make the difference between you or the thief owning the gun.

The trunk was once a good place, but today most cars come with a trunk-opening latch or button in the passenger compartment. A gun stored in the trunk must also be in a locked container. It is impossible to discreetly store a handgun in a trunk.

When traveling, stay at hotels with in-room safes or bring a Secure-It. The key point is this: when you are carrying or storing in public, maintaining control of your weapon is your responsibility. It needs to be either on your person, or secured.

That is just plain good common sense, and good safety.

Number and type of guns carried

Wisconsin law does not limit the number of handguns, electronic control devices, knives, and billy clubs or combinations thereof that a license holder may carry. Most people will carry their weapon of choice and leave it at that. At most, you may want to consider a back up weapon along with your primary weapon.

Handguns vs. long guns

In terms of carrying a firearm under Wisconsin's license law, a license holder may only carry a handgun in public. They may not carry rifles or shotguns in public. Under constitutional carry, firearms (including long guns) may be carried openly. Constitutional carry is subject to compliance with other state laws and regulations. Except for a short list of exceptions, long guns must be unloaded and incased for transport by everyone.

When a person is on or in property they own or lease, any type of firearm that they are lawfully allowed to possess may be carried.

And remember: a gun never solves problems.

Chapter 10
Gun Safety, On and Off the Range

Safety is a vital component of LEOSA Trainers, Inc. and therefore, this book's orientation. The safety rules are simple, practical, and important and in some cases elegant. Any one of the rules can save you from having a very bad experience with your handgun. When these rules become second nature, the chance of making what could be a very regrettable error lessens.

Armed citizens especially need to make a firm commitment to obey *all* the rules, *all* the time. If you make following the rules a habit all of the time, the odds that you will ever unintentionally hurt someone with your handgun is close to zero. Virtually all, if not completely all, negligent discharges can be traced back to at least one safety rule being broken. We can safety say that all negligent discharges were avoidable.

We are focused on handguns; however there is a simple fact that applies to *all* firearms: after a bullet leaves the barrel, there is no way to call it back. You own the bullet from the time it leaves the muzzle until it stops moving. Your first objective against causing legal harm to yourself is to make sure no bullet is ever fired from your gun unless you intend for it to happen. Your second objective is to make sure that, even if a bullet is fired unintentionally, it will cause the least amount of harm possible.

The safety rules are designed to support these objectives. This is why habitualizing the rules is so important. No one should get hurt and nothing should get destroyed so long as you make a habit of living the rules.

Basic safety rules

The four basic safety rules are straightforward. We have changed their original order for the simple reason that you cannot verify a firearm is unloaded until you have picked it up. While checking it, it must be pointed in some direction, so we address the rules in the order in which you must perform them.

1. Always keep your finger outside the trigger guard until you are ready to shoot

People seem to have more trouble with this rule than any other because of the ergonomics of handguns. The very function of a handgun requires they be designed for the trigger finger to naturally want to land on the trigger. This is why you must train and make a habit of keeping your finger outside of the trigger  guard until you have a target acquired and are ready to shoot.

It is extremely important to keep your trigger finger pointed straight forward and parallel with the barrel. It is important that you keep your finger off the trigger, even when the gun is pointed at a target, until you are actually ready to shoot. Until then, you have no reason to touch the trigger.

This rule has benefits beyond safety in a defensive shooting situation. Keeping your finger along the frame allows the finger to act as an aiming aid. Your eyes are on target. Your finger is naturally pointing where your eyes are focused. With your finger resting parallel to the barrel the handgun, the gun will shoot where your finger was pointed and where you are looking. By pointing your trigger finger at the target, you improve your accuracy. Your hand-eye coordination replaces using your sights for aiming.

A second benefit to keeping your finger outside of the trigger guard is that it gives you an opportunity to make the final shoot-no-shoot decision. Under the stress of an attack, once you put your finger on the trigger, it is highly likely you will fire the gun. Keeping your finger off the trigger until the last possible moment allows for a better decision to shoot or not.

2. Keep your firearm pointed in a safe direction

Whenever you are carrying a handgun, make sure the muzzle never points at anything you are not willing to destroy. Even when holstering a handgun, do it without pointing the muzzle toward any part of your own or anyone else's body.

Muzzle control has to be done consciously at first. You are holding an unloaded handgun with it pointed in a safe direction when somebody walks in front of it. You must take the responsibility to make sure it does not point at that person. The moment you perceive the muzzle may point at the person walking, you need to move the muzzle to a new safe direction. This must be actively practiced until it becomes second nature. Muzzle awareness can become so habitual that you will automatically know to reposition the muzzle even when distracted by a conversation.

So what is a safe direction? There are two ways to discern a safe direction. First, an unsafe direction is one in which you would not intend the firearm to be fired (discharged). You recognize something or someone in the possible path of the bullet that you do not want to destroy or injure. Second, a safe direction is any direction that should the firearm discharge at that moment, the least possible amount of damage would occur. A safe direction can be a matter of degree. Unless the firearm is aimed downrange at a shooting range, rarely is there a 100% safe direction. So a determination must be made as to the safest direction available at that moment.

3. Every firearm is loaded until proven unloaded

The main cause of negligent discharges is someone did not verify if a firearm was loaded or not and just assumed that the handgun was in a safe state. If you make it a policy to perform a clearing procedure every time you handle a handgun, even when you are certain that you unloaded and cleared it already you will never have a negligent discharge. It is impossible for an unloaded firearm to unintentionally fire.

Since LEOSA Trainers, Inc.'s primary focus is self-defense training, we know that all self-defense handguns are always loaded. Therefore, we alter this rule to say that *every gun is loaded until you prove it is unloaded*. To do this, you perform a clearing procedure (more on that in a moment).

Negligent discharges are a failure to do what a prudent individual would have otherwise done. The handgun went bang when you did not expect it to go bang. This means one or more safety rules were broken. It is a negligent discharge whether or not someone was injured or something got damaged. The degree of damage caused is a function of how many other safety rules were broken.

Accidental discharges are a mechanical failure of the firearm or ammunition and not a failure of the operator to follow the safety rules. Accidental discharges are very rare.

4. Always know your target and what is beyond it

From a defensive gun use standpoint, there is no reason to ever draw your handgun without a clear understanding of the threat and of your target. It is impossible to satisfy the law regarding privilege without a clear threat and therefore an identified target. Even when you have an identified target, it does not mean you can just start shooting. You must satisfy the tactical issues, one of which is what is beyond your target? The shoot-no shoot decision requires you to consider, if you can, if the bullet you shoot at the target will hurt an innocent bystander.

In the real world, when it comes down to saving your life what is beyond your target is probably not going to matter. You have to shoot and you will shoot. Add to this the fear and stress of having to defend yourself and all of a sudden, how well you have psychologically prepared yourself, how well you have trained with your handgun, how competent and poised you have become will make owning the results of shooting someone more survivable.

Of course, the best way to avoid needing to "know what is beyond your target" is to not let yourself get into the situation. That takes being situationally aware of your physical situation, as well as your options, so you can plan ahead. Get in the habit of thinking through the possible costs and benefits of drawing your gun before a situation ever presents itself. "Be prepared" is not just a motto for scouts.

Rules for handling guns

Beyond the four basic safety rules, the next in importance are the rules for handling firearms.

Let's take each in turn.

Clearing procedures

New gun owners need to learn what experienced gun owners have made a habit. Every time a handgun is picked up a clearing procedure must be performed by opening actions and checking firearms. The well trained gun owner is not forgetful or nervous, they are just practicing good handgun safety. Even if you have just handed an unloaded gun to your best friend he should perform a clearing procedure verifying that the handgun is unloaded. The moment he hands it back to you, you must open the action and verify it is unloaded. Although this appears redundant, and maybe even silly, developing the habit of performing a clearing procedure every time you touch a handgun is fundamental to safely living with firearms. Your verifying whether a handgun is loaded trumps all the other safety rules in preventing a negligent discharge.

Revolver clearing procedure

For revolvers, it is a matter of swinging out the cylinder, at which point the revolver, even if the cylinder is loaded, cannot fire, and looking into each chamber. If the chambers contain a casing, use the ejector rod to remove the casing. It can be difficult to determine whether the chambered case is a live round or a spent case until it has been removed from the chamber. A dimple in the primer from the firing pin does not guarantee the round is spent. Although simple, opening the cylinder and emptying the chambers is a two-step clearing procedure. Be sure to consult the owner's manual for instruction on the operation of your revolver.

Semiautomatic clearing procedure

Semiautomatics are more complicated because they can have rounds in the magazine, in the chamber, or both. It is important to follow all the steps, *in this order*, every time:

1. First, remove the magazine, and either set it aside.
2. Second, rack the slide *three times*. Pull the slide all the way back

and let it go. Do not worry about doing it gingerly; the gun can handle it. If a round is ejected after the first racking, you failed to do step one. Remove the magazine and rack the pistol three more times.

3. Third, pull the slide all the way back, and if so equipped, lock the slide in the open position. Inspect the chamber to be sure it is empty.

4. Fourth, if the slide does not lock open make the action inert by pointing the pistol in a safe direction and press the trigger with chamber empty.

Be sure to consult the owner's manual for instruction on the operation of your semiautomatic.

This is the same semiautomatic clearing procedure taught to air marshals, federal flight deck officers (armed pilots), and other federal law-enforcement officers. It works for them. Make it work for you, too.

If you uncock the gun by pulling the trigger without verifying that the chamber is empty, you may put a hole in something. This is a negligent discharge. *Do not make this unfortunate error!*

Almost everyone who has seen a cartridge ejected from a supposedly unloaded pistol has experienced a momentary surge of adrenaline and a big dose of humility.

Handing a handgun to another person

Before you hand a firearm to someone else, make it a point to verify that the gun is unloaded and the action is open.

A revolver with an empty cylinder swung out, or a semiautomatic with the slide locked back and the magazine removed, simply can't fire at that moment. The base if the grip should be pointed at the person receiving the handgun with the barrel pointed in the safest direction.

Make it a habit, when handing a firearm to somebody else, to do it just like this. In addition to being the safest way to hand off a firearm, it also shows consideration and respect for the recipient.

If somebody wants to hand you a firearm, ask them to unload it and open the action

There are very few situations when this rule and the rule above do not apply.

Do not leave firearms unattended, loaded or not

The reasons for this are obvious. Firearms that are not under your immediate control should be secured. If they are not being kept for self-protection, they should be unloaded as well. Many states, Wisconsin included have laws regarding leaving a handgun assessable to minors

Think before you act—take your time

If you are at the range, and your handgun has failed to fire when you have pressed the trigger, there is no reason at all to rush. Keep the handgun pointed down range and wait at least fifteen seconds before attempting to clear the misfire. If you are concerned or unsure about what to do next, call the range officer or a knowledgeable friend over.

Safety when shooting

Beyond gun handling are issues around actually shooting. Most shooting, of course, should and will take place on the range.

Wear safety glasses and hearing protection

This should be obvious, but we will say it anyway: loud sharp sounds can severely damage your hearing. Be sure to have your hearing protection in place *before* you step out on the range. Hearing protection can consist of specially made earplugs or headsets that clamp over the ears. In some cases, wearing both is preferable.

There are also very effective electronic sound-canceling headsets that use high-tech computer circuitry to cancel out loud sounds while letting ordinary sounds like conversation through.

Lead particles and flying brass can be bad for your eyes. For those who do not wear glasses normally, eye protectors are necessary. For those who do, eye protectors that fit over glasses add protection and are strongly recommended.

Be sure you know where your bullet will go

The range is the place to learn how to make your firearm shoot where you aim it or point it. Before selecting a particular handgun for carry, be sure it points well for you. If a particular handgun shoots to the right of where you aim or point it, you want to find that out at the shooting range and not in the street.

Formal ranges have massive backstops behind the target area. Even so, at indoor ranges, note that the ceiling above the target is often marred by bullets that did not go where they were supposed to.

At an indoor range, that is careless shooting and likely to irritate the range owner. Outdoors, it can be much worse. A round that is fired above the backstop can go a long distance. Most well-designed outdoor ranges have a large enough "dead area" behind the backstop, that is often not the case with informal ranges. Be sure that you know where your bullet is going to go, not only if you hit the target, but if you miss it.

Do not carry or shoot when impaired

This should be obvious.

An afternoon at the range, followed by dinner and a few drinks with friends is a fine thing, just as a few beers around the cabin or campfire after a day of hunting is.

It is *the order* that is important. Reverse the order, drink before shooting and you are asking for trouble. Guns and alcohol just do not mix, and that includes while cleaning them as well as shooting them.

The same thing obviously applies to any drug (prescription or non-prescription) that affects your judgment or perception. We're not suggesting any silliness here. Mixing firearms and impairing (whether of the legal or illegal variety) drugs is not only illegal, it is stupid.

Remember that many nonprescription drugs contain alcohol and that some can affect judgment and perception. Some common antihistamines can have a dramatic effect. Any medication with the warning "do not operate heavy equipment" or "may cause drowsiness" anywhere on the bottle should be a clue that you should stay away from your firearms while using that medication. If in any doubt, do not carry or go shooting until you have consulted with a physician or pharmacist.

A few miscellaneous safety issues:

Wash your hands

The chemical components that make up modern propellants are not very toxic, but they are not intended for human consumption. Eating the lead in bullets is very definitely toxic. After shooting, be sure to wash your hands thoroughly before doing anything else.

Cleaning guns

For whatever reason, negligent discharges and cleaning a gun just seem to go together. In every case one or more the four basic safety rules were violated (most likely a failure to perform clearing procedure). So before beginning any cleaning session perform a clearing procedure on firearms you intend to clean.

When it is time to clean, a firearm be sure to consult the owner's manual for instruction on how to disassemble your firearm and review the manufacturer's recommendations for cleaning.

Do not ignore safety rules. As you move from firearm to firearm for cleaning make sure it is unloaded and remove any ammunition from the immediate area.

Cleaning a firearm is a great time to introduce children to your handgun. They can look at components normally hidden and ask questions to better understand how each part makes the handgun work. If you are lucky, they will help you clean the handgun.

Storage at home

Firearms that are not being kept for self-defense should be unloaded and secured, with the ammunition stored separately. For those owning a lot of firearms, make it easy on yourself by owning a gun safe. Buy the biggest safe you have room for because as soon as it is home and installed it will be too small. For those with only a few guns (at least for now), buy good gun cases (preferably lockable) and store them in a locked closet.

When it comes to self-defense weapons, storage options are less obvious and require some careful thought. Self-defense firearms need to be stored loaded. Your specific household circumstances will determine your options. Accounting for kids in your life is the foremost concern. If you do not have kids to worry about leaving your handgun on the nightstand is perfectly okay. A self-defense handgun is a "working gun" when it is in its holster and being carried. A stored self-defense handgun is a working handgun that is "off-the clock." So, the trick is to store your handgun so it can be easily retrieved and get "back on the clock" as quickly as possible if needed. If a handgun is needed, *it is needed now.*

There is a Texas saying, "I live by the eight foot rule. I'm never more than eight feet from a loaded gun." Storing several firearms throughout your home is a good way to go. Making them accessible for you and not for others again requires the proper storage equipment. Quick access handgun safes, bed rail mounted shotgun racks, under the bathroom sink lockboxes, under the towel rack and behind the towel, handgun storage wall clocks, hollow books, lockbox inside of the lazy boy or behind a suitable curtain are all storage ideas that work. Firearms can be discretely stored for quick access and with the safety of children in mind.

And, as a matter of safe gun handling, every time you remove the handgun from the box be sure to check whether or not it is loaded. Yes, you will treat it as loaded regardless, but you do need to know, not remember or assume.

Gun safety and children

For those with children, the most important part of gun safety is education. Teaching your children the gun safety rules for children is essential.

The NRA "Eddie Eagle" program recommends teaching children to do the following if they see a firearm:

STOP!
DO NOT touch.
LEAVE the area.
TELL an adult.

We recommend the NRA "Eddie Eagle" program very strongly. With hundreds of millions of firearms in tens of millions of households in the US, it is important for all children to know what to do if they see a firearm: *Stop! Do not touch. Leave the area. Tell an adult.* This training will be useful not only in your own home, but can save a life should your children visit the home of someone who pays less attention to safety than you do. Two unsupervised children and a firearm is a very dangerous situation. Your child should be taught to immediately leave, come home and tell you what happened.

Teaching children about the proper handling of firearms under an adult's supervision is certainly a good idea. Take your children to the range and teach them range rules. Have kids observe adults shooting provide the opportunity to point out good behavior and occasionally less than good behavior. Children experiencing the sound of shooting and recoil will impress upon them the power of firearms. Finally, letting them shoot an appropriate caliber firearm for their age, size, and experience will properly begin a lifelong relationship with firearms.

And remember, a gun never solves problems.

LEOSA Trainers, Inc.

Chapter 11
Shooting, on the Range and on the Street

When you take your carry license course from a LEOSA Trainers, Inc., instructor, shooting should be a relatively small but an important part of your training.

The reason is simple: Carrying a firearm is 95% between your ears and 5% in the holster. Most of what is important about the responsibilities of a license holder are the day-to-day things: staying out of trouble, avoiding conflict, and so forth. Most license holders, as we have said, will never have to so much as take out their handgun "for real" and that is just fine.

But if you are going to carry a self-defense handgun, you must be competent and know how to shoot it. While we are going to discuss some of the details of that here, you really do need some one-on-one instruction if you are not already very familiar with handguns. Even then, more instruction is a good idea.

This is not to say that LEOSA Trainers, Inc. is the only group whose certified instructors can teach beginners about safe gun handling and basic shooting skills. There are also many gun clubs in Wisconsin that give introductory courses in firearms handling and shooting, and they are generally very good.

However, there is a very large difference between target shooting, the focus of most handgun courses, and self-defense shooting training, which is the concern of LEOSA Trainers, Inc. License to Carry training.

Target shooting vs. self-defense shooting

Target shooting is, among other things, fun and for some a very competitive sport. At a range, you stand behind a shooting bench in a well-lighted area shooting at a target that is anywhere from 5 to 25 yards down range. You take your time settling into whatever position you like, take a breath and let half of it out, focus carefully on the sights and gently press the trigger until the gun fires. If you have done it right, there is a nice round hole in the paper target, or perhaps you have knocked over a tin can, or turned a stale cookie into a cloud of rapidly expanding crumbs.

The point is that when target shooting you can take your time, are not under real stress, and can easily see not only your target, but also your sights.

A self-defense shooting is going to be *different* in almost every respect. Most self-defense shootings take place with a distance between victim and attacker of no more than ten feet and under low-light conditions. At ten feet or less shooting the attacker center of mass will not require sights. Self-defense shootings start and end very quickly, often within ten seconds or less so there is not a lot of time for thought. If you have a lot of time to think, you have enough time to escape.

The stress of a life-threatening situation causes physiological changes that have serious implications. It is not possible to duplicate the actual stress of a life-threatening event on the shooting range.

What is possible to do is teach self-defense shooting, as opposed to target shooting. We start with how you stand, moving to how you hold your firearm, to how you aim (point) it (and we emphasize *point* when shooting in self-defense) and how many times to fire your handgun.

Studies and review of actually DGU's have shown that under the stress of a life threatening situation police and armed citizens use what is known as an Isosceles stance combined with point shooting.

The Natural Isosceles

The Isosceles is instinctive. You face the target squarely. You may find yourself taking at least a half set backwards. This is a natural reaction to a threat. In fact, moving backwards, or any other direction, will make you a

more difficult target for your attacker. Moving backwards indicates your desire to get away and any witnesses will more likely see you as the victim.

The handgun is thrust out using both arms equally, either at chest or eye level, as though using the gun to push the threat away.

A violent confrontation is physiologically different than shooting on the range. A massive adrenaline dump and the sudden stress of close personal violence makes it almost impossible for most people to use the sights or focus on anything other than the threat.

If your attacker is also moving taking an accurate shot becomes even more difficult. You will have control over stopping momentarily when you shoot, but your attacker is not going to be that cooperative.

Leveraging the body's natural response to a threat makes your response easier. So integrating this natural response with your training at the range makes your response to the threat more fluid, faster, and automatic. Do not mistake this as an excuse not to train. We are just being smarter about it

Colonel Rex Applegate, who spent much of WWII training OSS agents, argued over many years that, "most shooters, no matter how well trained in other stances instinctively revert to the Isosceles when faced with life threatening situations.

Videos of police shootings bear this out. Police are, by and large, *not* trained to step back, and they *are* trained to use their sights. Nevertheless, in video after video, you can see that the officers are stepping back and focusing on the attacker instead of their sights.

This is why we emphasize that your carry handgun must *point* well for you. *Point shooting is aimed shooting.* You are just using your body, hand eye coordination, and stance to aim at the target rather than the sights of your gun.

The late Julio Santiago of Burnsville, Minnesota, a veteran of the US Army and twenty-five years as a Deputy Sheriff, was one of the first trainers to note this. He spent much of his life teaching the importance of point shooting, particularly in low-light situations where the sights won't be useful.

Most self-defense shootings take place at very close distances where point shooting works. Beyond close range, distance yields time, and with that maybe you can escape without having to fire. If you can safely escape, you should.

Take a look around your home. Unless your house has very large rooms, it is difficult to envision a situation where you could be more than 20 or so feet away from an attacker.

This is why self-defense firearms training takes place at very close distances. Many LEOSA Trainers, Inc. trainers do all their shooting training and qualifications between 15 and 21 feet which, in terms of real-life self-defense distances, is fairly long.

You should regularly plan range time, at least once a month. Shooting skills are a depreciable skills so regular practice is required. Using formal or informal instruction is a good idea. Practice using the Isosceles stance.

To assume an Isosceles stance, grip the handgun with your strong hand (finger off the trigger) and support it with your weak hand. Bring it up to chest level and thrust it straight out toward the target, as though trying to push it away with the muzzle of the firearm. Look at the target and not your sights. You should be square with the target, your feet at shoulder width or more.

If the pistol fits your hand correctly, when you shoot, a hole will appear near the middle of the target, what would be the center of mass of an attacker. If you keep firing in this way, a number of holes will appear near the center of the target.

It is aimed fire with your body and stance doing the target aiming. It is really that simple.

If you want to use the sights, just raise the handgun to eye level. Most people will need to turn their heads slightly to bring the dominant eye in line with the sights, but do not close the other eye. You will not do it in a self-defense situation, and it is best to practice what you would actually do.

Most people, of course, simply won't be able to focus on the sights. Look at the picture on the right. Would you be looking at your sights or at the attacker?

The Weaver

In the Weaver stance, the body is turned slightly away from the target as the pistol is brought up to eye level so that the sights can be used in a two handed grip, with the strong arm flexed and the weak arm flexed more. The strong arm pushes out on the pistol, while the weak arm pulls in, creating an isometric clamp on the handgun that helps the shooter quickly return the pistol to the same position after each shot. It feels a little awkward at first, but with some practice it is possible to quickly fire multiple accurate shots at a target.

The Chapman

The Chapman stance, or Modified Weaver, is similar. The main difference is that the strong arm is kept as straight as possible, ideally with the elbow locked. In effect, the strong arm becomes a human rifle stock. Again, the strength of the upper body is used to bring the sights back on target, and the target is not faced quite directly.

With either the Weaver or the Chapman stance, the torso is at 60 to 90 degrees away from the target and head is usually turned slightly to the side to bring the dominant eye in line with the sights.

There is no question that mastering either of these stances requires a lot of time and effort. The problem is that many people (we think almost all) who have been thoroughly trained in either of these stances simply won't use it when under the stress of an attack.

What could go wrong?

You have not trained sufficiently and when under the stress of an attack have nothing to rely on. Confusion reigns and even the smallest tasks become huge obstacles. Do not find yourself betwixt and between half sight-shooting, half point-shooting, and mostly missing. Commit to regular practice and practice correctly using your natural response to a threat and the shooting skills taught by your instructor. Train yelling, "Stop, don't hurt me! Stop, don't hurt me!"

You have a handgun that doesn't fit your hand. Either you bought the wrong gun or someone gave you're the wrong gun. Point shooting requires a handgun that fits your hand. There will not be time for "grip adjustment" in the middle of an attack.

If you flinch your shots, they will be wildly off target. If flinching is your problem, it can be corrected by dry firing your handgun and focusing on keeping the front sight center target and the back sights properly aligned. As you dry fire, your front sight need to remain on target and properly aligned with the back sights. Stop anticipating the recoil. Focus on the trigger press.

Practicing

License holders should make practice a regular part of their lives at least once a month and more often is better.

But *what* you practice is as important as *how often* you practice. Plinking at long-distance targets with a .22 target pistol can be fun, but it is not self-defense practice.

Practice at realistic self-defense distances. Four feet to twenty-one feet are good self-defense ranges. Some ranges may have a minimum distance greater than four feet. Follow the minimum range rule.

Most people will instinctively take up a stance similar to the Natural Isosceles stance, with the handgun thrust out at chest level, and that is what we think most of you should practice. Fire two center of mass shots and a third to the hip area and assess. For some sequences, fire a second set of three rounds to stop the threat.

When you are under stress you will resort to your training. Remember, rational thought is difficult so training to fire three rounds and evaluate is what you will do on the street. However, if you train to empty the magazine or until the revolver goes "click" that is what you will probably do in a defensive gun use. You are shooting to stop the treat and only the minimum number of rounds necessary to stop the threat is considered reasonable force. Too few and the threat continues. Too many and its murder. The difference between going home and going to prison can be nothing more than how many times you pressed the trigger.

Your practice shooting should consist of three center-of-mass shots with one of the three shots to the pelvis. After three shots, evaluate your attacker's condition. You are looking for a change in condition. Is the change noticeable? Are the notice changes sufficient to believe the threat has stopped? If the first three shots have done enough damage to convince you that the threat is passed then you must cease fire. If you evaluate the threat as present and continuing, three more shots are called for.

Practice often.

And remember: a gun never solves problems.

Sheepdogs must continually train.

CHAPTER 12
Training

If you have decided to pursue a Wisconsin weapons license, your next step should be to get training. Although not required by law, we believe appropriate training will keep you out of prison, so it is required by common sense. LEOSA Trainers's training will include both classroom training and a shooting qualification. After you pass the course, you will be presented with a certificate of training making you eligible to apply for a Wisconsin license.

Qualifications

To get a Wisconsin carry license, you need to meet the training qualifications. What is necessary to qualify for a Wisconsin license and what is needed to stay out of prison is not necessarily the same thing. LEOSA Trainers, Inc. teaches what it believe is necessary to stay out of prison and to be reasonably competent with a handgun.

Where to get training

Under the WPPA, there is a wide variety of training meeting the law's requirements. We recommend LEOSA Trainers, Inc. curriculum because it has been accredited by a number of states and/or their respective Law Enforcement organizations.

What training consists of

LEOSA Trainers, Inc. believes that training to carry lethal force for personal protection requires much more than knowing how to hunt or serve your country in the military. Our job is to provide the instruction necessary for you to survive a defensive gun use legally, physically, and morally. Frankly other acceptable forms of training will not do this.

And remember: a gun never solves problems.

Chapter 13
Out-of-State Licenses

The Wisconsin legislature has set minimum standards in the WPPA regarding the recognition of out of state permits. The one sure requirement is that the state of issue must do a background check. This should mean that almost all permits or licenses to carry will be recognized by Wisconsin. Wisconsin residents can only carry in Wisconsin under a Wisconsin license to carry. The Wisconsin Department of Justice will publish a list of states Wisconsin recognizes.

Out-of-state licenses for Wisconsin Residents

Getting an out-of-state license also serves as a workaround for some Wisconsin residents. If you travel and your favorite destination state does not recognize your Wisconsin license you still have some options.

Many other states have had concealed carry laws for years. The agreements are already in place for most of these states regarding recognition (one state automatically honors another's licenses) or reciprocity with each other (each state must recognize the other for the licenses to be valid in the other state). On a rare occasion a state may terminate recognition of another states license. Consult www.handgunlaw.us or the Attorney General's office of the state where you plan to travel through or visit.

Sometimes it takes awhile for a new state law to be recognized by other states. Formal agreements may need be made. Other times reluctant government officials will not do anything until someone insists. Still other officials will not act to support law-abiding license holders because they do not like guns and do not want to see carry laws expanded in any way.

Several states will allow you to apply by mail without having to leave Wisconsin. The four obvious options, are Pennsylvania, Florida, New Hampshire, and Utah. To remain timely, we again want to refer you to www.handgunlaw.us for application details for non-resident permits.

And remember: a gun never solves problems.

CHAPTER 14
What to Do After You Have Your License

First of all, of course, *stay out of trouble*.

Look at it this way: most people who get licenses have already gone their entire lives without needing to point a gun at another human being and it is obviously best to keep it that way. If you have not been persuaded by the previous chapters about the use of lethal force and what happens after a defensive gun use, even if you have not so much as pointed it at anybody, read them again.

The carry license simple allows you to carry a concealed weapon in public. It does not make you bulletproof, attack-proof, arrest-proof, or lawsuit-proof or a junior G-man.

And of all the many things it is not, the foremost among them is a reason to go looking for trouble.

Spend time at the range with your carry handgun

A handgun is a tool. As with most tools, the more you use it, the more poised and competent you become with it, and the more likely that even under stress you will use it properly. Particularly at first you should plan on making regular trips to the range and practicing point-shooting at close targets. Practice as if you were in a real DGU; three shots and evaluate.

Clean your carry handgun

Handguns are machines, and machines need regular care and maintenance. People adopt different policies about how often and how thoroughly to clean their handguns. Some take the position that the handgun should be clean enough to "eat off of" and perform a full, detailed disassembly and cleaning of their guns after every shooting session. That is not wrong, although it might be excessive.

After a detailed cleaning of a handgun, we recommend at least dry firing it to be sure it functions properly.

We recommend a minimum cleaning by swabbing the barrel, wiping the breach area with a lightly oiled cloth patch between full breakdown cleanings. Remember, do not over oil.

Keep up with changes in the law

There will be issues that Wisconsin courts and perhaps the legislature will need to address. You can expect there to be test cases to define the scope of the WPPA. The only way you ever want to be involved in a test case, of course, is to read about it.

There is the legislature. As Judge Gideon J. Tucker said in 1866, "No man's life, liberty, or property is safe while the legislature is in session." There are elements of the Wisconsin law that need to be clarified by the legislature. Other states have had to do this. There is also the temptation of the gun control proponents to erode the law or to add back restrictions. Enacting the WPPA is only the beginning of having to protect the gains that have been made. It is important to keep a watchful eye on the legislature.

Prepare to renew your license

There is no rush; your license is valid for five years. It is a really good idea to take a refresher course because the law can change and, when acting in self-defense, you must be right in your decision to use lethal force. Over time, there may also be principles and rules you have forgotten.

The Wisconsin DOJ has created a website specifically to make it easy for people to either apply for a new license or to renew their license. Other routine administrative matters such as changing a name, requesting a replacement license can also be completed through this website. If you have any questions, it also has a FAQ page. The website address is https://concealedcarry.doj.wi.gov/#! . No less than 90 days before the expiration date of the license, the Department of Agriculture and Consumer Services shall mail to each licensee a written notice of the expiration and a renewal form prescribed by the Department of Agriculture and Consumer Services.

The licensee must renew his or her license on or before the expiration date by filing with the Department of Agriculture and Consumer Services the renewal form containing a notarized affidavit stating that the licensee remains qualified pursuant to the criteria specified in 790.06 subsections (2) and (3), a color photograph as specified in paragraph (5) (e), and the required renewal fee. Out-of-state residents must also submit a complete set of fingerprints and fingerprint processing fee.

The license shall be renewed upon receipt of the completed renewal form, color photograph, appropriate payment of fees, and, if applicable, fingerprints.

Additionally, a licensee who fails to file a renewal application on or before its expiration date must renew his or her license by paying a late fee of $15.

A license may not be renewed 180 days or more after its expiration date, and such a license is deemed to be permanently expired.

A person whose license has been permanently expired may reapply for licensure; however, an application for licensure and fees under subsection (5) must be submitted, and a background investigation shall be conducted pursuant to this section. A person who knowingly files false information under this subsection is subject to criminal prosecution under § 837.06.

You should take a refresher course because things do change. Perhaps your initial training was not as good as you expected so this is an opportunity to correct that, or bring a friend or family member who wants to apply for their Wisconsin license.

Contact your LTI instructor for more information about the renewal process.

And, for one last time, remember:

a gun never solves problems.

GLOSSARY

ACP

An abbreviation for "Automatic Colt Pistol" which is used to denote certain ammunition such as 25 ACP, 32 ACP, 380 ACP, and 45 ACP.

ACTION

A term used to describe what happens to the hammer when the trigger is pressed. A single action firearm must first be manually cocked and the trigger simply releases the trigger to fire. A double action means when the trigger is pressed, the hammer is both cocked and then released.

AFFIRMATIVE DEFENSE

An admission or "affirmation" that the act was indeed committed, but that the actor was justified or privileged in doing what would otherwise be criminal, because they acted in self-defense.

To successfully convict the actor of the crime, the prosecution must prove to the court beyond a reasonable doubt that the actor truly did not act in self-defense. This sets the standard to convict the actor, at the highest level.

The actor carries the benefit of assumption, which means he does not need any evidence to support his claim. However, if the prosecution can fulfill their burden of proof, the benefit of assumption shifts away from the actor, who now has to prove their claim, or be found guilty.

AIRGUN

A gun that used a spring, compressed air or other gas to propel a projectile.

AMMUNITION

Except for muzzle loading firearms, typically this will be a cartridge for pistols and rifles and shells for shotguns consisting of a case holding a primer, a charge (guncotton), and a projectile (a bullet, slug or buckshot).

APPROVED FIREARMS SAFETY COURSES

1. The hunter education program established under Wisconsin statute s. 29.591 or a substantially similar program that is established by another state, country, or province and that is recognized by the department of natural resources.
2. A firearms safety or training course that is conducted by a national or state organization that certifies firearms instructors.
3. A firearms safety or training course that is available to the public and is offered by a law enforcement agency or, if the course is taught by an instructor who is certified by a national or state organization that certifies firearms instructors or by the department, by a technical college, a college or a university, a private or public institution or organization, or a firearms training school.
4. A firearms safety or training course that is offered to law enforcement officers or to owners and employees of licensed private detective and security agencies.
5. A firearms safety or training course that is conducted by a firearms instructor who is certified by a national or state organization that certifies firearms instructors or who is certified by the department.

APPROVED EVIDENCE OF TRAINING

1. Documentation that the individual completed military, law enforcement, or security training that gave the individual experience with firearms that is substantially equivalent to a course or program
2. A current or expired license, or a photocopy of a current or expired license, that the individual holds or has held that indicates that the individual is licensed or has been licensed to carry a firearm in this state or in another state or in a county or municipality of this state or of another state unless the license has been revoked for cause.
3. Documentation of completion of small arms training while serving in the U.S. armed forces, reserves, or National Guard as demonstrated by an honorable discharge or general discharge under honorable conditions or a certificate of completion of basic training with a service record of successful completion of small arms training and certification.

ASSAULT RIFLE

These are a select fire rifle (semi auto and full auto) of intermediate power. The semi automatic varieties that are cosmetically similar are not assault rifles.

AUTOMATIC FIRE (full auto)

A firearm that can repeat the firing cycle of multiple cartridges with one press of the trigger.

BACKGROUND CHECK

This means the search the Department of Justice conducts to determine a person's eligibility for a license to carry a concealed weapon.

BALLISTICS

This is the science of studying moving projectiles and attention can be either focused on what happens inside a firearm, what happens after a bullet leaves the firearm or both.

BALL

This can mean a round ball projectile used in a muzzle loading firearm, or more commonly, to describe bullets that have a solid round or pointed nose.

BILLY CLUB

Either a collapsible or solid club made from wood, metal or plastic that can be used to strike another person.

BLOWBACK ACTION

What is common to all blowback systems is that the cartridge case must move under the direct action of the powder pressure, therefore any gun in which the bolt is not rigidly locked and permitted to move while there remains powder pressure in the chamber will undergo a degree of blowback.

The cycle begins when the cartridge is fired. Expanding gases from the fired round send the projectile down the barrel and at the same time applies force to the case against the breech face of the bolt, overcoming the inertia of the bolt, resulting in a "blow back" effect. The breech is kept sealed by the cartridge case until the bullet has left the barrel and gas pressure has dropped to a safe level; the inertia of the bolt mass ensures this (mass of the bolt + recoil spring, in some cases the hammer force too). As the bolt travels back, the spent cartridge case is extracted and then ejected, and the firing mechanism is cocked. The action spring then propels the bolt forward again, which strips a round from the feed system along the way. The bolt carries a new cartridge into the chamber

This system is only suitable for firearms using relatively low pressure cartridges. Pure blowback operation is typically found on semi-automatic, small-caliber pistols and rifles.

BORE
The inside of a firearms barrel.

BRASS
Typically used to describe a used cartridge case, no matter what material it is actually made.

BREECH
The place where a bullet is inserted into a gun near the rear of the barrel. It is also called a chamber. The breech is not a part of the barrel.

BULLET
This is the projectile that comes out of the firearm.

CALIBER
The diameter of either a projectile of the barrel of a firearm. Firearms are measured from the lands, ammunition may be measured from either the lands or the groves (.38 special is measured from the groves, .357 magnum is measured from the lands). This can be measured in hundreds of an inch (.38), thousands of an inch (.380) or millimeters (9mm).

CARRY
Means to go armed with.

CARTRIDGE
One complete round of ammunition.

CASE
For handguns and rifles, this is the metal part of the cartridge that holds the primer, propellant and bullet.

CCW
An abbreviation that can mean concealed carry weapon or to carry concealed weapon. It is also used to denote a permit or license to carry, even in states like Wisconsin where concealed carry is not required by law.

CENTER FIRE
This describes a type of cartridge or shotgun shell, with the primer positioned in the center of the base.

CLERK
This is a clerk of the circuit court or, if it has enacted a law or an ordinance in conformity with Wisconsin statute s. 346.63, the clerk of the court for a federally recognized American Indian tribe or band in this state, a city, a village, or a town.

CLIP
This is not the magazine that supplies ammunition to a firearm!

This is a straight or round device that holds a number of cartridges together at the base. The ammunition may be stripped or pushed off the clip into a magazine to load it quickly. A round device may be used to hold revolver cartridges for quick loading into the cylinder.

COP-KILLER BULLET
A term used by the media to scare the women and horses. Conversely, there are no bullets that are non-cop-killer. Bullets do not exercise discretion over their targets.

COURT AUTOMATED INFORMATION SYSTEMS

This means the information system under Wisconsin statute s.758.19 (4).

CYLINDER

Sometimes referred to as the wheel of a revolver, this is the part of the firearm that holds the ammunition supply and turns as each cartridge is fired to supply another round.

CYLINDER GAP

This is the distance between the cylinder and the barrel of a revolver. It should not be greater that the thickness of a piece of writing paper. The gap between the cylinder and the frame near the firing pin should not be greater than a business card.

CYLINDER STOP

This is a little metal device that is extended typically up from the frame in a revolver to lock the cylinder in place so the ammunition is properly aligned in the cylinder with both the firing pin to the rear and the barrel to the front of the gun.

DANGEROUS WEAPON

Wisconsin statutes define a dangerous weapon as follows: "Dangerous weapon" means any firearm, whether loaded or unloaded; any device designed as a weapon and capable of producing death or great bodily harm; any ligature or other instrumentality used on the throat, neck, nose, or mouth of another person to impede, partially or completely, breathing or circulation of blood; any electric weapon, as defined in Wisconsin statute s. 941.295 (4) (1c) (a); or any other device or instrumentality which, in the manner it is used or intended to be used, is calculated or likely to produce death or great bodily harm.

DAO

This is an acronym for double action only firearms. When the trigger is pressed, the trigger first cocks the hammer, and when the trigger is pressed further, releases the hammer to strike the firing pin to discharge the cartridge.

DEPARTMENT
This refers to the Wisconsin Department of Justice.

DESTRUCTIVE DEVICE
This has the meaning given in 18 USC 921 (a) (4).

DGU
An acronym for a defensive gun use. If the four elements are all present, the odds of your surviving physically, emotionally, legally and financially improve greatly.

EJECTOR
Just as a bouncer ejects some patrons when it is time to leave the bar, this little device ejects the spent case from a semi automatic's chamber to make it ready to place a fresh round in the chamber.

ELECTRONIC CONTROL DEVICE
An electronic control device or electric weapon means any device which is designed, redesigned, used or intended to be used, offensively or defensively, to immobilize or incapacitate persons by the use of electric current. It may also be used to temporarily subdue a person to create an opportunity to escape from him or her. It is unlikely this device will stop an attack by itself because that is not what it is designed to do.

ENCASED
This means enclosed in a case that is expressly made for the purpose of containing a firearm and that is completely zipped, snapped, buckled, tied or otherwise fastened with no part of the firearm exposed.

EXTRACTOR
This is a little hook that grabs the spent case and pulls it out of the chamber so the ejector can send it flying down the shirt of the person (usually a woman) standing beside you.

FIREARM
A handgun, rifle, or shotgun that uses gunpowder or guncotton as a propellant.

FIREARM SILENCER

This has the meaning given in Wisconsin Statute s. 941.298 (1).

FMJ

A bullet that is covered by a metal cover or coating.

FORMER FEDERAL LAW ENFORCEMENT OFFICER

Means a person who separated from service as a law enforcement officer at a federal law enforcement agency and who resides in Wisconsin.

FORMER LAW ENFORCEMENT OFFICER

Means a person who separated from service as a law enforcement officer from a state or local law enforcement agency in Wisconsin.

FPE

This is an acronym for Foot Pounds of Energy.

FPS

This is an acronym for Feet Per Second. It is the common measurement for the speed of a bullet

FTE

This means a Failure to Fire. It can be the result of operator error, ammunition or a mechanical failure of the firearm.

GAP

This is new ammunition introduced for some Glock pistols, the .45 caliber GAP cartridge is a shorter length than the more common .45 ACP cartridge.

GRIP

This is the portion of the pistol or revolver that is held by either hand when shooting.

GRIP SAFETY

In some pistols, there is a strap running along the rear of the grip that must be depressed before the pistol will fire.

GUNPOWDER

Gunpowder is also known as black powder and is a mixture of sulphur, charcoal and potassium nitrate. Gunpowder was discovered in the 9th century by the Chinese who were searching for an elixir of immortality. This discovery led to the invention of fireworks and the earliest gunpowder weapons in China.

SMOKELESS POWDER

Smokeless powder refers to propellants used in firearms and artillery, which produce negligible smoke when fired. Older forms of gunpowder produced significant amounts of smoke.

There are several types of smokeless powder which include Cordite, Ballistite and, historically, Poudre B. Smokeless powders fall into one of three major classifications: single-base, double-base or triple-base powders.

Smokeless powder consists of nitrocellulose (single-base powders), are frequently combined with up to 50 percent nitroglycerin (double-base powders), and sometimes are combined with nitroglycerin and nitroguanidine (triple-base). The powder is formed into small spherical balls, extruded cylinders or flakes.

Double-base propellants commonly propel handgun and rifle ammunition. Triple-base propellants commonly propel artillery guns.

HALF COCKED

A position when the hammer is pulled back but before being fully cocked, that it is held in place and can not strike the firing pin.

HAMMER BLOCK

A hammer safety that keeps the hammer away from the firing pin unless the trigger is pulled.

HAMMER SPUR

The rear part of a hammer you use to cock the hammer with your thumb.

HAMMERLESS

The firearm really has a hammer, but it is enclosed within the frame.

HANDGUN

Means any weapon designed or redesigned, or made or remade, and intended to be fired while held in one hand and to use the energy of an explosive to expel a projectile through a smooth or rifled bore. A handgun does not include a machine gun, as defined in Wisconsin statute s. 941.27 (1), a short barreled rifle, as defined in Wisconsin statute s. 941.28 (1) (b), or a short barreled shotgun, as defined in Wisconsin statute s. 941.28 (1) (c).

HANGFIRE

This is an ammunition malfunction that results in either no bang or a delayed bang. If this happens to you, it is a good idea to keep the handgun pointed in a safe direction for 10 to 15 seconds until you know which version you have.

HARM

"Bodily harm" means physical pain or injury, illness, or any impairment of physical condition.

"Substantial bodily harm" means bodily injury that causes a laceration that requires stitches, staples, or a tissue adhesive; any fracture of a bone; a broken nose; a burn; a petechia; a temporary loss of consciousness, sight or hearing; a concussion; or a loss or fracture of a tooth.

"Great bodily harm" means bodily injury which creates a substantial risk of death, or which causes serious permanent disfigurement, or which causes a permanent or protracted loss or impairment of the function of any bodily member or organ or other serious bodily injury.

HIGH CAPACITY MAGAZINE

During the Clinton gun ban era, any magazine that held more than 10 rounds was considered a high capacity magazine. This term has outlived it's useful life.

HOLLOW POINT

A bullet designed to expand to about twice its original diameter upon impact. This is a good self-defense choice because it makes a bigger permanent cavity causing more trauma, and is less likely to over penetrate the bad guy and enter the wrong person.

IMMUNITY

(a) When acting in good faith under this section, the department and its employees and a law enforcement agency and its employees are immune from civil and criminal liability arising from any act or omission under this section.

(b) When acting in good faith under this section, an entity providing firearms training to comply with the requirements of the WPPA law under sub. (2) (a) 2., (3) (a) 2., or (5) and its employees are immune from civil and criminal liability arising from any act or omission that is related to that training.

(c) A person that does not prohibit an individual from carrying a concealed weapon on property that the person owns or occupies is immune from any liability arising from its decision.

(d) An employer that does not prohibit one or more employees from carrying a concealed weapon under sub. (15m) of the WPPA is immune from any liability arising from its decision.

IWB

This is a holster worn "inside the waistband" of pants or shorts for concealed carry.

JHP

This is a hollow point that has a metal jacket around the bullet.

LAW ENFORCEMENT AGENCY

(1) An agency that consists of one or more persons employed by the federal government, including any agency described under 18 USC 926C (e) (2);

(2) A state, or a political subdivision of a state;

(3) The U.S. armed forces;

(4) or the National Guard, that has as its purposes the prevention and detection of crime and the enforcement of laws or ordinances, and that is authorized to make arrests for crimes.

Law enforcement agency does not include the Wisconsin Department of Justice.

LAW ENFORCEMENT OFFICER

Means a person who is employed by a law enforcement agency for the purpose of engaging in, or supervising others engaging in, the prevention, detection, investigation, or prosecution of, or the incarceration of any person for, any violation of law and who has statutory powers of arrest.

LEO

Law Enforcement Officer or anyone with arresting authority.

LEOSA

The acronym for the federal Law Enforcement Officers Safety Act enacted by Congress in 2004 which created two classes of law enforcement officers who could carry a concealed firearm in any state or political subdivision. The classes are "qualified law enforcement officers" and "retired or separated law enforcement officers". There are two types of laws not overridden by this Federal law. They are state laws which prohibit or restrict the possession of firearms on any State or local government property, installation, building, base, or park and state laws as respects the gun free school zones.

LICENSEE

is a Wisconsin resident who holds a valid license to carry a concealed weapon issued under this section.

LTC

License to Carry a weapon in Wisconsin either openly or concealed.

MACHINE GUN

This weapon has the meaning given in Wisconsin statute s. 941.27 (1).

MAGAZINE

This is not a clip!

For pistols, this is a detachable holder for the ammunition supply. It may be a single stack which is slightly larger than the width of the ammunition, or a double stack which is wider because it loads the ammunition nearly side by side for greater ammunition capacity. These are placed in the firearm in a space inside the grip.

MAGAZINE SAFETY

Some pistols can not be fired if the magazine has been removed. Maybe.

MAGNUM

Think super sized. More power, more kick, more damage, and may be more difficult to control.

MOTOR VEHICLE

Has the meaning given in Wisconsin statute s. 340.01 (35).

MUZZLE

The muzzle is the business end of the barrel from which the bullet exits.

MUZZLE BLAST

This is the concussion at the muzzle from the expansion of gasses after the bullet leaves the barrel. At very close range, with larger calibers or magnum loads, the muzzle blast can be as damaging as the bullet. This is the "close counts" factor.

MUZZLE FLASH

Rarely noticed when shooting outside during the daylight hours, this can be blinding to the shooter when shooting in the dark. It is a bright flash from the expulsion of burning propellant after the bullet exits the barrel.

NONRESIDENTIAL BUILDING

A nonresidential building includes a nursing home as defined in Wisconsin statute s. 50.01 (3), a community based residential facility as defined in Wisconsin statute s. 50.01 (1g), a residential care apartment complex as defined in Wisconsin statute s. 50.01 (1d), an adult family home as defined in Wisconsin statute s. 50.01 (1), and a hospice as defined in Wisconsin statute s. 50.90 (1).

NONRESIDENTIAL BUILDING POSTING

While carrying a firearm, enters or remains in any part of a nonresidential building, grounds of a nonresidential building, or land that the actor does not own or occupy after the owner of the building, grounds, or land, if that part of the building, grounds, or land has not been leased to another person, or the occupant of that part of the building, grounds, or land has notified the actor not to enter or remain in that part of the building, grounds, or land while carrying a firearm or with that type of firearm.

This does not apply to a part of a building, grounds, or land occupied by the state or by a local governmental unit, to a privately or publicly owned building on the grounds of a university or college, or to the grounds of or land owned or occupied by a university of college, or, if the firearm is in a vehicle driven or parked in the parking facility, to any part of a building, grounds, or land used as a parking facility.

OUT OF BATTERY

When the slide, bolt or cylinder is out of position and the firearm can not be fired.

OUT-OF-STATE LICENSE

An out-of-state license means a valid permit, license, approval, or other authorization issued by another state if all of the following apply:

1. The permit license, approval, or other authorization is for the carrying of a concealed weapon.

2. The state is listed in the rule promulgated by the department under Wisconsin statute s. 165.25 (12) and, if that state does not require a background search for the permit, license, approval, or authorization, the permit, license, approval, or authorization designates that the holder chose to submit to a background search.

OUT-OF-STATE LICENSEE

An out-of-state licensee means an individual who is 21 years of age or over, who is not a Wisconsin resident, and who has been issued an out-of-state license.

OWB

A hip holster that is worn on the outside of the pants or shorts.

PARABELLUM

The ammunition designed to be used in the German Lugar P 08 pistol. It is now used to denote the 9 mm cartridge used in most 9mm pistols.

PHOTOGRAPHIC IDENTIFICATION CARD

This means one of the following:

1. An operator's license issued under ch. 343 or an identification card issued under Wisconsin statute s. 343.50.
2. A license or card issued by a state other than Wisconsin that is substantially equivalent to a Wisconsin operators license or card.

PISTOL

A firearm designed to be fired using one hand or two hands. Although the meaning includes a revolver, it is most often used to refer to a semi automatic handgun.

PRIMER

The point of contact on a bullet where the firing pin or hammer strikes, that contains an ignition material.

QUALIFIED OUT-OF-STATE LAW ENFORCEMENT OFFICER

This is a law enforcement officer to whom all of the following apply:

1. The person is employed by a state or local government agency in another state.
2. The agency has authorized the person to carry a firearm.
3. The person is not the subject of any disciplinary action by the agency that could result in the suspension or loss of the person's law enforcement authority.
4. The person meets all standards established by the agency to qualify the person on a regular basis to use a firearm.
5. The person is not prohibited under federal law from possessing a firearm.

RECEIVER

Also called the frame, it is the part of the firearm that holds everything (the grip, barrel, breech or chamber, slide, bolt) together.

182

RECOIL

For every action, there is an equal and opposite reaction. This is the force applied against the shooter from the ignited cartridge (in the case of a revolver it is also the "feel" of the maximum impact of a bullet on a target, at the muzzle).

RESIDENCE

1. With respect to a single-family residence, includes the residence building and the parcel of land upon which the residence building is located; and
2. With respect to a residence that is not a single-family residence, does not include any common area of the building in which the residence is located or any common areas of the rest of the parcel of land upon which the residence building is located.

REVOLVER

A pistol that uses a cylinder to hold the ammunition supply which rotates (or revolves) with each trigger press to position the next cartridge to be fired.

RIFLING

This is found inside of a barrel and consists of "lands" which are raised and twisted, and the groves between the lands. The effect is to put a spin (like a football) on the bullet as it moves down the barrel to improve accuracy.

RIMFIRE

The most common rimfire cartridge is the .22 caliber. The primer is coated within the entire rim so it does not matter where the firing pin strikes the rim.

SA

Short for single action, the trigger only releases the hammer. The trigger will not cock the hammer, you must do that manually.

SAFETY

Any mechanical device that will prevent a firearm from firing a cartridge. They sometimes fail so do not totally trust them.

SCHOOL ZONE

Property that is within 1,000 feet of the grounds of a school, not from the school building itself.

SEAR

The thing that holds either a hammer or striker cocked.

SEMI-AUTOMATIC

A firearm that requires a separate press of the trigger, to fire each and every round.

SHEEP

Generally, a good person who is incapable of violence. These people do not ever see the need for defensive weapons because they believe the police are there to protect them. To cope, sheep must live in a world of denial. To recognize reality would require them to examine and perhaps question their fundamental belief systems, and they will not allow that.

SHEEPDOG

This refers to people who are also good people, but are capable of violence if sufficiently provoked. Sheepdogs are not mean people or bullies, but they understand that random acts of violence could find them and are willing to use force stop a threat against their life if it becomes necessary.

SNUB NOSE

This is a handgun (usually a revolver) with a short barrel, usually two inches or less.

SPECIAL EVENT

A special event for license holders means an event that is open to the public, is for a duration of not more than 3 weeks, and either has designated entrances to and from the event that are locked when the event is closed or requires an admission.

STANDARD OF PROOF

This is the standard of proof needed to convince a court that any given claim is true. The degree of proof necessary can depend upon the seriousness of the charge, the circumstances of the alleged crime, or the type of crime being charged. There are three standards typically applied in Wisconsin.

1. Beyond a Reasonable Doubt is the highest standard and is most often used in criminal trials. It requires a not-guilty verdict if there is any reasonable doubt of the facts presented by the prosecution.
2. Clear and Convincing is the next highest level and is mid way between the lowest and highest levels of proof. This standard is typically used in civil trials.
3. Preponderance of the Evidence is the lowest standard of proof and is a greater than 50% threshold of guilt. It is the standard normally applied in civil trials and Grand Jury indictment proceedings.

STATE IDENTIFICATION CARD NUMBER

A state identification card number means the unique identifying driver number assigned to a person by the department of transportation under Wisconsin statute s. 343.17 (3) (a) 4, or, if the person has no driver number, the number assigned to the person on an identification card issued under Wisconsin statute s. 343.50.

SUBMACHINE GUN

This is a full auto firearm that typically uses pistol ammunition for close quarter shooting. The Auto Ordinance "Tommy Gun" is among the most famous submachine guns and uses .45 ACP ammunition (although it is available in a semiautomatic version which is also a lot of fun to shoot).

TRANSFER BAR

This is a safety feature found on some revolvers that rises into the firing position when the trigger is pulled. It is what actually hits or "transfers" the force of the hammer to the firing pin.

TRIGGER

When pressed, it either cocks and releases, or just releases the hammer (or striker). It may also disengage (or engage as with a transfer bar) a safety device.

TRIGGER GUARD

This is a metal guard that surrounds the trigger, usually by connecting the grip and frame, and is designed to protect the trigger from being moved backward.

WEAPON

According to Wisconsin state law, these are devices that a person with a license to carry, may possess while in public. They include a handgun, an electric weapon, as defined in Wisconsin statute s. 941.295 (1c) (a), a knife other than a switchblade knife under Wisconsin statute s. 941.24, or a billy club.

WISCONSIN PERSONAL PROTECTION ACT

An unofficial name used to refer to the Wisconsin carry law (Act 35, 2011 legislative session). This law preserves constitutional open carry, and open carry or concealed carry for license holders. It authorizes the carry of handguns, electronic control devices, billy clubs and knives (not switchblades).

WOLF

This is a person who has become an animal. They will kill other people just for the sport of it. They have no moral compass and are not concerned with the consequences of the judicial system. Wolves just need to be shot.

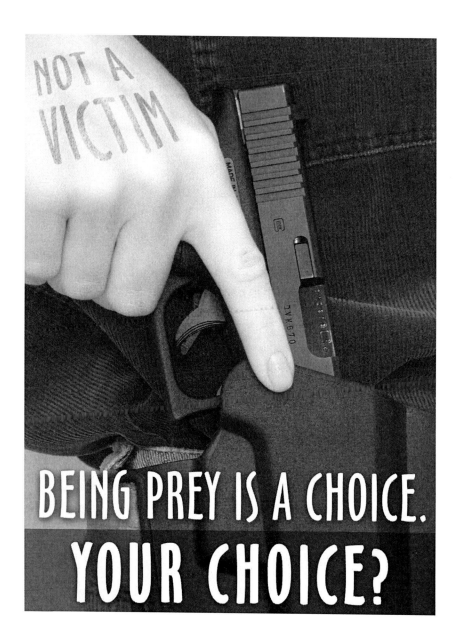

Appendix A
Necessary Equipment

Carrying a handgun is not, or shouldn't be, just a matter of having a handgun and carry license. We think there are several other items that a license holder should definitely have, and others that are a good idea to have, depending on your budget.

Required equipment

- A reliable handgun that points well for you.
- A pocket holster, or some other carry method or combination of carry methods that works for you throughout Wisconsin's varying seasons.
- Your carry license, and driver's license or State issued I.D.
- A cell phone.
- A digital recorder, lockable, with 2 gig minimum storage
- A storage box or some other method to secure your firearm, whether you are out in public or at home, should you need to.

- A gun cleaning kit.
- The phone number of a good criminal lawyer.

Recommended equipment

- A flashlight. (We recommend a Xenon flashlight, available at www.aacfi.com/products/XenonFlashlight.shtml)
- A spare handgun.
- A spare magazine for a semiauto, or a speedloader for a revolver.
- A spare wallet containing some expired credit cards and around $20 in small bills—you can throw it to a mugger as you run in the opposite direction.

Appendix B

Wisconsin Statute 175.60
License to carry a concealed weapon

As amended effective 2015

175.60   License to carry a concealed weapon.

(1) **Definitions.** In this section:

(ac) "Background check" means the searches the department conducts under sub. (9g) to determine a person's eligibility for a license to carry a concealed weapon.

(ag) "Carry" means to go armed with.

(b) "Department" means the department of justice.

(bm) "Handgun" means any weapon designed or redesigned, or made or remade, and intended to be fired while held in one hand and to use the energy of an explosive to expel a projectile through a smooth or rifled bore. "Handgun" does not include a machine gun, as defined in s. 941.25 (1), a short-barreled rifle, as defined in s. 941.28 (1) (b), or a short-barreled shotgun, as defined in s. 941.28 (1) (c).

(bv) "Law enforcement agency" does not include the department.

(c   "Law enforcement officer" has the meaning given in s. 165.85 (2) (c).

(d   "Licensee" means an individual holding a valid license to carry a concealed weapon issued under this section.

(dm) "Military resident" means an individual who is in active service in the U.S. armed forces and is stationed in this state for a term that is scheduled to be at least one year in duration.

(e   "Motor vehicle" has the meaning given in s. 340.01 (35).

(f)   "Out-of-state license" means a valid permit, license, approval, or other authorization issued by another state if all of the following apply:

     1.   The permit, license, approval, or other authorization is for the carrying of a concealed weapon.

     2.   The state is listed in the rule promulgated by the department under s. 165.25 (16) and, if that state does not require a background search for the permit, license, approval, or authorization, the permit, license, approval, or authorization designates that the holder chose to submit to a background search.

(g)   "Out-of-state licensee" means an individual who is 21 years of age or over, who is not a Wisconsin resident, and who has been issued an out-of-state license.

(h)   "Photographic identification card" means one of the following:

     1.   An operator's license issued under ch. 343 or an identification card issued under s. 343.50.

     2.   A license or card issued by a state other than Wisconsin that is substantially equivalent to a license or card under subd. 1.

(i) "State identification card number" means one of the following:

     1.   The unique identifying driver number assigned to a Wisconsin resident by the department of transportation under s. 343.17 (3) (a) 4. or, if the Wisconsin resident has no driver number, the number assigned to the Wisconsin resident on an identification card issued under s. 343.50.

     2.   The unique identifying driver number assigned to a

military resident by the military resident's state or, if the military resident has no driver number, the number assigned to the military resident on an identification card issued by the military resident's state.

(j) "Weapon" means a handgun, an electric weapon, as defined in s. 941.295 (1c) (a), or a billy club.

(2) **Issuance and scope of license.**

(a) The department shall issue a license to carry a concealed weapon to any individual who is not disqualified under sub. (3) and who completes the application process specified in sub. (7). A license to carry a concealed weapon issued under this section shall meet the requirements specified in sub. (2m).

(b) The department may not impose conditions, limitations, or requirements that are not expressly provided for in this section on the issuance, scope, effect, or content of a license.

(c) Unless expressly provided in this section, this section does not limit an individual's right to carry a firearm that is not concealed.

(d) For purposes of 18 USC 922 (q) (2) (B) (ii), an out-of-state licensee is licensed by this state.

(2g) **Carrying a concealed weapon; possession and display of license document or authorization.**

(a) A licensee or an out-of-state licensee may carry a concealed weapon anywhere in this state except as provided under subs. (15m) and (16) and ss. 943.13 (1m) (c) and 948.605 (2) (b) 1r.

(b)

1. Unless the licensee is carrying a concealed weapon in a manner described under s. 941.23 (2) (e), a licensee shall have with him or her, during all times he or she is carrying a concealed weapon, his or her license document, photographic identification card, and, if the licensee is a military resident, his or her military license.

2. Unless the out-of-state licensee is carrying a concealed weapon in a manner described under s. 941.23 (2) (e), an out-of-state licensee shall have with him or her his or her out-of-state license and photographic identification card at all times during which he or she is carrying a concealed weapon.

(c) Unless the licensee or out-of-state licensee is carrying a concealed weapon in a manner described under s. 941.23 (2) (e), upon request by a law enforcement officer who is acting in an official capacity and with lawful authority, a licensee who is carrying a concealed weapon shall display to the officer his or her license document, photographic identification card, and, if the licensee is a military resident, his or her military license, and an out-of-state licensee who is carrying a concealed weapon shall display to the officer his or her out-of-state license and photographic identification card.

(2m) License document; content of license.

(a) Subject to pars. (b), (bm), (c), and (d), the department shall design a single license document for licenses issued and renewed under this section. The department shall complete the design of the license document no later than September 1, 2011.

(b) A license document for a license issued under this section shall contain all of the following on one side:

1. The full name, date of birth, and residence address of the licensee.

2. A physical description of the licensee, including sex, height, and eye color.

3. The date on which the license was issued.

4. The date on which the license expires.

5. The name of this state.

6. A unique identification number for each licensee.

(bm) The reverse side of a license document issued under this section shall contain the requirement under sub. (11) (b) that the licensee shall inform the department of any address change no later than 30 days after his or her address changes and the penalty for a violation of the requirement.

(c) The license document may not contain the licensee's social security number.

(d)

1. The contents of the license document shall be included in the document in substantially the same way that the contents of an operator's license document issued under s. 343.17 are included in that document.

2. The license document issued under this section shall be tamper proof in substantially the same way that the operator's license is tamper proof under s. 343.17 (2).

(e) The department of justice may contract with the department of transportation to produce and issue license documents under this section. Neither the department of transportation nor any employee of the department of transportation may store, maintain, or access the information provided by the department of justice for the production or issuance of license documents other than to the extent necessary to produce or issue the license documents.

(3) **Restrictions on issuing a license.** The department shall issue a license under this section to an individual who submits an application under sub. (7) unless any of the following applies:

(a) The individual is less than 21 years of age.

(b) The individual is prohibited under federal law from possessing a firearm that has been transported in interstate or foreign commerce.

(c) The individual is prohibited from possessing a firearm under s. 941.29.

(d) The court has prohibited the individual from possessing a dangerous weapon under s. 969.02 (3) (c) or 969.03 (1) (c).

(e) The individual is on release under s. 969.01 and the individual may not possess a dangerous weapon as a condition of the release.

(f) The individual is not one of the following:
1. A Wisconsin resident.
2. A military resident.

(g) The individual has not provided proof of training as described under sub. (4) (a).

(4) **Training requirements.**

(a) The proof of training requirement under sub. (7) (e) may be met by any of the following:

1. A copy of a document, or an affidavit from an instructor or organization that conducted the course or program, that indicates the individual completed any of the following:

a. The hunter education program established under s. 29.591 or a substantially similar program that is established by another state, country, or province and that is recognized by the department of natural resources.

b. A firearms safety or training course that is conducted by a national or state organization that certifies firearms instructors.

c. A firearms safety or training course that is available to the public and is offered by a law enforcement agency or, if the course is taught by an instructor who is certified by a national or state organization that certifies firearms instructors or by the department, by a technical college, a college or a university, a private or public institution or organization, or a firearms training school.

d. A firearms safety or training course that is offered to law enforcement officers or to owners and employees of licensed private detective and security agencies.

e. A firearms safety or training course that is conducted by a firearms instructor who is certified by a national or state organization that certifies firearms instructors or who is certified by the department.

2. Documentation that the individual completed military, law enforcement, or security training that gave the individual experience with firearms that is substantially equivalent to a course or program under subd. 1.

3. A current or expired license, or a photocopy of a current or expired license, that the individual holds or has held that indicates that the individual is licensed or has been licensed to carry a firearm in this state or in another state or in a county or municipality of this state or of another state unless the license has been revoked for cause.

4. Documentation of completion of small arms training while serving in the U.S. armed forces, reserves, or national guard as demonstrated by an honorable discharge or general discharge under honorable conditions or a certificate of completion of basic training with a service record of successful completion of small arms training and certification.

(b)

1. The department shall certify instructors for the purposes of par. (a) 1. c. and e. and shall maintain a list of instructors that it certifies. To be certified by the department as an instructor, a

person must meet all of the following criteria:

a. Be qualified under sub. (3) to carry a concealed weapon.

b. Be able to demonstrate the ability and knowledge required for providing firearms safety and training.

2. The department may not require firing live ammunition to meet the training requirements under par. (a).

(5) Application and renewal forms.

(a) The department shall design an application form for use by individuals who apply for a license under this section and a renewal form for use by individuals applying for renewal of a license under sub. (15). The department shall complete the design of the application form no later than September 1, 2011, and shall complete the design of the renewal form no later than July 1, 2014. The forms shall require the applicant to provide only his or her name, address, date of birth, state identification card number, race, sex, height, and eye color and shall include all of the following:

1. A statement that the applicant is ineligible for a license if sub. (3) (a), (b), (c), (d), (e), (f), or (g) applies to the applicant.

2. A statement explaining self-defense and defense of others under s. 939.48, with a place for the applicant to sign his or her name to indicate that he or she has read and understands the statement.

3. A statement, with a place for the applicant to sign his or her name, to indicate that the applicant has read and understands the requirements of this section.

4. A statement that an applicant may be prosecuted if he or she intentionally gives a false answer to any question on the application or intentionally submits a falsified document with the application.

5. A statement of the penalties for intentionally giving a false answer to any question on the application or intentionally submitting a falsified document with the application.

6. A statement of the places under sub. (16) where a licensee is prohibited from carrying a weapon, as well as an explanation of the provisions under sub. (15m) and ss. 943.13 (1m) (c) and 948.605 (2) (b) 1r. that could limit the places where the licensee may carry a weapon, with a place for the applicant to sign his or

her name to indicate that he or she has read and understands the statement.

(b) The department shall make the forms described in this subsection available on the Internet and, upon request, by mail.

(7) **Submission of application.** An individual may apply for a license under this section with the department by submitting, by mail or other means made available by the department, to the department all of the following:

(a) A completed application in the form prescribed under sub. (5) (a).

(b) A statement that states that the information that he or she is providing in the application submitted under par. (a) and any document submitted with the application is true and complete to the best of his or her knowledge.

(c) A license fee in an amount, as determined by the department by rule, that is equal to the cost of issuing the license but does not exceed $37. The department shall determine the costs of issuing a license by using a 5-year planning period.

(d) A fee for a background check that is equal to the fee charged under s. 175.35 (2i).

(e) Proof of training as described under sub. (4) (a).

(9) **Processing of application**

(a) Upon receiving an application submitted under sub. (7), the department shall conduct a background check.

(b) Within 21 days after receiving a complete application under sub. (7), the department shall do one of the following:

1. Issue the license and promptly send the licensee his or her license document by 1st class mail.

2. Deny the application, but only if sub. (3) (a), (b), (c), (d), (e), (f), or (g) applies to the applicant. If the department denies the application, the department shall inform the applicant in writing, stating the reason and factual basis for the denial.

(9g) **Background checks.**

(a) The department shall conduct a background check regarding an applicant for a license using the following procedure:

1. The department shall create a confirmation number associated with the applicant.

2. The department shall conduct a criminal history record search and shall search its records and conduct a search in the national

instant criminal background check system to determine whether the applicant is prohibited from possessing a firearm under federal law; whether the applicant is prohibited from possessing a firearm under s. 941.29; whether the applicant is prohibited from possessing a firearm under s. 51.20 (13) (cv) 1., 2007 stats.; whether the applicant has been ordered not to possess a firearm under s. 51.20 (13) (cv) 1., 51.45 (13) (i) 1., 54.10 (3) (f) 1., or 55.12 (10) (a); whether the applicant is subject to an injunction under s. 813.12 or 813.122, or a tribal injunction, as defined in s. 813.12 (1) (e), issued by a court established by any federally recognized Wisconsin Indian tribe or band, except the Menominee Indian tribe of Wisconsin, that includes notice to the respondent that he or she is subject to the requirements and penalties under s. 941.29 and that has been filed with the circuit court under s. 813.128 (3g); and whether the applicant is prohibited from possessing a firearm under s. 813.123 (5m) or 813.125 (4m); and to determine if the court has prohibited the applicant from possessing a dangerous weapon under s. 969.02 (3) (c) or 969.03 (1) (c) and if the applicant is prohibited from possessing a dangerous weapon as a condition of release under s. 969.01.

3. As soon as practicable, the department shall do the following:

a. If the background check indicates sub. (3) (b), (c), (d), or (e) applies to the applicant, create a unique nonapproval number for the applicant.

b. If the completed background check does not indicate that sub. (3) (b), (c), (d), or (e) applies to the applicant, create a unique approval number for the applicant.

(b) The department shall maintain a record of all completed application forms and a record of all approval or nonapproval numbers regarding background checks under this subsection.

(9r) **Emergency license.**

(a) An individual who requires an immediate license may petition the court in the county in which he or she resides for such a license. Unless the court knows that the individual is ineligible for a license under sub. (3), a court may issue an emergency license to an individual if the court determines that immediate licensure is warranted to protect the individual from death or great bodily harm, as defined in s. 939.22 (14).

(b) An emergency license issued under this subsection is valid for 30 days unless it is revoked under par. (bm) or it is void under par. (c).

(bm) If the court determines that a holder of an emergency license issued under par. (a) is ineligible under sub. (3) for a license, the court shall revoke the emergency license.

(c) If the holder of an emergency license issued under par. (a) applies for a license under sub. (7) and is determined to be ineligible under sub. (3) for a license, the emergency license is void.

(11) **Updated information.**

(a)

1. In this paragraph:

a. "Clerk" means the clerk of the circuit court or, if it has enacted a law or an ordinance in conformity with s. 346.63, the clerk of the court for a federally recognized American Indian tribe or band in this state, a city, a village, or a town.

b. "Court automated information systems" means the systems under s. 758.19 (4).

2. The court automated information systems, or the clerk or register in probate, if the information is not contained in or cannot be transmitted by the court automated information systems, shall promptly notify the department of the name of any individual with respect to whom any of the following occurs and the specific reason for the notification:

a. The individual is found by a court to have committed a felony or any other crime that would disqualify the individual from having a license under this section.

b. The individual is found incompetent under s. 971.14.

c. The individual is found not guilty of any crime by reason of mental disease or mental defect under s. 971.17.

d. The individual is involuntarily committed for treatment under s. 51.20 or 51.45.

e. The individual is found incompetent under ch. 54.

f. The individual becomes subject to an injunction described in s. 941.29 (1m) (f) or is ordered not to possess a firearm under s. 813.123 (5m) or 813.125 (4m).

g. A court has prohibited the individual from possessing a dangerous weapon under s. 969.02 (3) (c) or 969.03 (1) (c).

h. A court has ordered the individual not to possess a firearm under s. 51.20 (13) (cv) 1., 51.45 (13) (i) 1., 54.10 (3) (f) 1., or 55.12 (10) (a).

i. The individual is on release under s. 969.01 and the individual may not possess a dangerous weapon as a condition of the release.

3. Upon receiving a notice under subd. 2., the department shall immediately determine if the individual who is the subject of the notice is a licensee, using the list maintained under sub. (12) (a).

(b)

1. No later than 30 days after changing his or her address, a licensee shall inform the department of the new address. The department shall include the individual's new address in the list under sub. (12) (a).

2. Except as provided in subd. 3., for a first violation of subd. 1., the department must issue the licensee a warning.

3. If an individual is in violation of subd. 1. and his or her license has been suspended or revoked under sub. (14), the individual is subject to the penalty under sub. (17) (ac).

4. A licensee may not be charged with a violation of subd. 1. if the department learns of the violation when the licensee informs the department of the address change.

(12) **Maintenance, use, and publication of records by the department.**

(a) The department shall maintain a computerized record listing the names and the information specified in sub. (2m) (b) of all individuals who have been issued a license under this section and all individuals issued a certification card under s. 175.49 (3). Subject to par. (b) 1. b., neither the department nor any employee of the department may store, maintain, format, sort, or access the information in any way other than by the names, dates of birth, or sex of licensees or individuals or by the identification numbers assigned to licensees under sub. (2m) (b) 6.

(b)

1. A law enforcement officer may not request or be provided information under par. (a) concerning a specific individual except for one of the following purposes:

a. To confirm that a license or certification card produced by an individual at the request of a law enforcement officer is valid.

b. If an individual is carrying a concealed weapon and claims to hold a valid license issued under this section or a valid certification card issued under s. 175.49 (3) but does not have his or her license document or certification card, to confirm that the individual holds a valid license or certification card.

c. To investigate whether an individual submitted an intentionally false statement under sub. (7) (b) or (15) (b) 2.

d. To investigate whether an individual complied with sub. (14) (b) 3.

2. A person who is a law enforcement officer in a state other than Wisconsin may request and be provided information under subd. 1. a. and b.

(c) Notwithstanding s. 19.35, the department of justice, the department of transportation, or any employee of either department may not make information obtained under this section available to the public except in the context of a prosecution for an offense in which the person's status as a licensee or holder of a certification card is relevant or through a report created under sub. (19).

(12g) **Providing licensee information to law enforcement agencies.**

(a) The department shall provide information concerning a specific individual on the list maintained under sub. (12) (a) to a law enforcement agency, but only if the law enforcement agency is requesting the information for any of the following purposes:

1. To confirm that a license or certification card produced by an individual at the request of a law enforcement officer is valid.

2. If an individual is carrying a concealed weapon and claims to hold a valid license issued under this section or a valid certification card issued under s. 175.49 (3) but does not have his or her license document or certification card, to confirm that an individual holds a valid license or certification card.

3. If the law enforcement agency is a Wisconsin law enforcement agency, to investigate whether an individual submitted an intentionally false statement under sub. (7) (b) or (15) (b) 2.

(b)

1. Notwithstanding s. 19.35, neither a law enforcement agency nor any of its employees may make information regarding an individual that was obtained from the department under this subsection available to the public except in the context of a prosecution for an offense in which the person's status as a licensee or holder of a certification card is relevant.

2. Neither a law enforcement agency nor any of its employees may store or maintain information regarding an individual that was obtained from the department under this subsection based on the individual's status as a licensee or holder of a certificate card.

3. Neither a law enforcement agency nor any of its employees may sort or access information regarding vehicle stops, investigations, civil or criminal offenses, or other activities involving the agency based on the status as licensees or holders of certification cards of any individuals involved.

(13) **Lost or destroyed license.** If a license document is lost, a licensee no longer has possession of his or her license, or a license document is destroyed, unreadable, or unusable, a licensee may submit to the department a statement requesting a replacement license document, the license document or any portions of the license document if available, and a $12 replacement fee. The department shall issue a replacement license document to the licensee within 14 days of receiving the statement and fee. If the licensee does not submit the original license document to the department, the department shall terminate the unique approval number of the original request and issue a new unique approval number for the replacement request.

(14) **License revocation, suspension, and surrender.**

(a) The department shall revoke a license issued under this section if the department determines that sub. (3) (b), (c), (e), (f), or (g) applies to the licensee.

(am) The department shall suspend a license issued under this section if a court has prohibited the licensee from possessing a dangerous weapon under s. 969.02 (3) (c) or 969.03 (1) (c). If the individual whose license was suspended is no longer subject to the prohibition under s. 969.02 (3) (c) or 969.03 (1) (c), whichever is applicable, sub. (3) (b), (c), (d), (e), (f), or (g) does not apply to the individual, and the suspended license would not have expired under sub. (15) (a) had it not been suspended, the department shall restore the license within 5 business days of notification that the licensee is no longer subject to the prohibition.

(b)

1. If the department suspends or revokes a license issued under this section, the department shall send by mail the individual whose license has been suspended or revoked notice of the suspension or revocation within one day after the suspension or revocation.

2. If the department suspends or revokes a license under this section, the suspension or revocation takes effect when the individual whose license has been suspended or revoked receives the notice under subd. 1.

3. Within 7 days after receiving the notice, the individual whose license has been suspended or revoked shall do one of the following:

a. Deliver the license document personally or by certified mail to the department.

b. Mail a signed statement to the department stating that he or she no longer has possession of his or her license document and stating the reasons why he or she no longer has possession.

(c) A military resident who holds a license shall surrender the license at the time he or she ceases to be stationed in this state.

(14g) **Departmental review.** The department shall promulgate rules providing for the review of any action by the department denying an application for, or suspending or revoking, a license under this section.

(14m) **Appeals to the circuit court.**

(a) An individual aggrieved by any action by the department denying an application for, or suspending or revoking, a license under this section, may appeal directly to the circuit court of the county in which the individual resides without regard to whether the individual has sought review under the process established in sub. (14g).

(b) To begin an appeal under this subsection, the aggrieved individual shall file a petition for review with the clerk of the applicable circuit court within 30 days of receiving notice of denial of an application for a license or of suspension or revocation of a license. The petition shall state the substance of the department's action from which the individual is appealing and the grounds upon which the individual believes the department's action to be improper. The petition may include a copy of any records or documents that are relevant to the grounds upon which the individual believes the department's action to be improper.

(c) A copy of the petition shall be served upon the department either personally or by registered or certified mail within 5 days after the individual files his or her petition under par. (b).

(d) The department shall file an answer within 15 days after being served with the petition under par. (c). The answer shall include a brief statement of the actions taken by the department. The department shall include with the answer when filed a copy of any documents or records on which the department based its action.

(e) The court shall review the petition, the answer, and any records or documents submitted with the petition or the answer. The review under this paragraph shall be conducted by the court without a jury but the court may schedule a hearing and take testimony.

(f) The court shall reverse the department's action if the court finds any of the following:

1. That the department failed to follow any procedure, or take any action, prescribed under this section.

2. That the department erroneously interpreted a provision of law and a correct interpretation compels a different action.

3. That the department's action depends on a finding of fact that is not supported by substantial evidence in the record.

4.

a. If the appeal is regarding a denial, that the denial was based on factors other than the factors under sub. (3).

b. If the appeal is regarding a suspension or revocation, that the suspension or revocation was based on criteria other than those under sub. (14) (a) or (am).

(g)

1. The court's decision shall provide whatever relief is appropriate regardless of the original form of the petition.

2. If the court reverses the department's action, the court may order the department to pay the aggrieved individual all court costs and reasonable attorney fees.

(15) **License expiration and renewal.**

(a) Except as provided in par. (e) and sub. (9r) (b), a license issued under this section is valid for a period of 5 years from the date on which the license is issued unless the license is suspended or revoked under sub. (14).

(b) The department shall design a notice of expiration form. At least 90 days before the expiration date of a license issued under this section, the department shall mail to the licensee a notice of expiration form and a form for renewing the license. The department shall renew the license if, no later than 90 days after the expiration date of the license, the licensee does all of the following:

1. Submits a renewal application on the form provided by the department.

2. Submits a statement reporting that the information provided under subd. 1. is true and complete to the best of his or her knowledge and that he or she is not disqualified under sub. (3).

4. Pays all of the following:

a. A renewal fee in an amount, as determined by the department by rule, that is equal to the cost of renewing the license but does not exceed $12. The department shall determine the costs of renewing a license by using a 5-year planning period.

b. A fee for a background check that is equal to the fee charged under s. 175.35 (2i).

(c) The department shall conduct a background check of a licensee as provided under sub. (9g) before renewing the licensee's license under par. (b).

(d) The department shall issue a renewal license by 1st class mail within 21 days of receiving a renewal application, statement, and fees under par. (b).

(e) The license of a member of the U.S. armed forces, a reserve unit of the armed forces, or the national guard who is deployed overseas while on active duty may not expire until at least 90 days after the end of the licensee's overseas deployment unless the license is suspended or revoked under sub. (14).

(15m) Employer restrictions.

(a) Except as provided in par. (b), an employer may prohibit a licensee or an out-of-state licensee that it employs from carrying a concealed weapon or a particular type of concealed weapon in the course of the licensee's or out-of-state licensee's employment or during any part of the licensee's or out-of-state licensee's course of employment.

(b) An employer may not prohibit a licensee or an out-of-state licensee, as a condition of employment, from carrying a concealed weapon, a particular type of concealed weapon, or ammunition or from storing a weapon, a particular type of weapon, or ammunition in the licensee's or out-of-state licensee's own motor vehicle, regardless of whether the motor vehicle is used in the course of employment or whether the motor vehicle is driven or parked on property used by the employer.

(16) Prohibited activity.

(a) Except as provided in par. (b), neither a licensee nor an out-of-state licensee may knowingly carry a concealed weapon, a weapon that is not concealed, or a firearm that is not a weapon in any of the following places:

1. Any portion of a building that is a police station, sheriff's office, state patrol station, or the office of a division of criminal investigation special agent of the department.

2. Any portion of a building that is a prison, jail, house of correction, or secured correctional facility.

3. The facility established under s. 46.055.

4. The center established under s. 46.056.

5. Any secured unit or secured portion of a mental health institute under s. 51.05, including a facility designated as the Maximum Security Facility at Mendota Mental Health Institute.

6. Any portion of a building that is a county, state, or federal courthouse.

7. Any portion of a building that is a municipal courtroom if court is in session.

8. A place beyond a security checkpoint in an airport.

(b) The prohibitions under par. (a) do not apply to any of the following:

1. A weapon in a vehicle driven or parked in a parking facility located in a building that is used as, or any portion of which is used as, a location under par. (a).

2. A weapon in a courthouse or courtroom if a judge who is a licensee is carrying the weapon or if another licensee or out-of-state licensee, whom a judge has permitted in writing to carry a weapon, is carrying the weapon.

3. A weapon in a courthouse or courtroom if a district attorney, or an assistant district attorney, who is a licensee is carrying the weapon.

(17) Penalties.

(a) Any person who violates sub. (2g) (b) or (c) may be required to forfeit not more than $25, except that the person shall be exempted from the forfeiture if the person presents to the law enforcement agency that employs the requesting law enforcement officer, within 48 hours, his or her license document or out-of-state license, photographic identification, and, if pertinent, military license.

(ac) Except as provided in sub. (11) (b) 2., any person who violates sub. (11) (b) 1. may be required to forfeit $50.

(ag) Any person who violates sub. (2m) (e), (12), or (12g) may be fined not more than $500 or sentenced to a term of imprisonment of not more than 30 days or both.

(ar) Any law enforcement officer who uses excessive force based solely on an individual's status as a licensee may be fined not more than $500 or sentenced to a term of imprisonment of not more than 30 days or both. The application of the criminal penalty under this paragraph does not preclude the application of any other civil or criminal remedy.

(b) Any person who violates sub. (16) may be fined not more than $500 or imprisoned for not more than 30 days or both.

(c) An instructor of a training course under sub. (4) (a) who intentionally submits false documentation indicating that an individual has met the training requirements under sub. (4) (a) may be prosecuted for a violation of s. 946.32.

(e) Any person required under sub. (14) (b) 3. to relinquish or deliver a license document to the department who intentionally violates the requirements of that subdivision shall be fined not more than $500 and may be imprisoned for not more than 30 days or both.

(18) Reciprocity agreements. The department may enter into reciprocity agreements with other states as to matters relating to licenses or other authorization to carry concealed weapons.

(19) Statistical report. By March 1 of each year, the department shall submit a statistical report to the legislature under s. 13.172 (2) and to the governor that indicates the number of licenses applied for, issued, denied, suspended, and revoked under this section during the previous calendar year. For the licenses denied, the report shall indicate the reasons for the denials and the part of the application process in which the reasons for denial were discovered. For the licenses suspended or revoked, the report shall indicate the reasons for the suspensions and revocations. The department may not include in the report any information that may be used to identify an applicant or a licensee, including, but not limited to, a name, address, birth date, or social security number.

(21) **Immunity.**

(a) The department of justice, the department of transportation, and the employees of each department; clerks, as defined in sub. (11) (a) 1. a., and their staff; and court automated information systems, as defined under sub. (11) (a) 1. b., and their employees are immune from liability arising from any act or omission under this section, if done so in good faith.

(b) A person that does not prohibit an individual from carrying a concealed weapon on property that the person owns or occupies is immune from any liability arising from its decision.

(c) An employer that does not prohibit one or more employees from carrying a concealed weapon under sub. (15m) is immune from any liability arising from its decision.

(d) A person providing a firearms training course in good faith is immune from liability arising from any act or omission related to the course if the course is one described in sub. (4) (a).

Appendix C
Milwaukee 1000ft School Zones (estimated 2006)

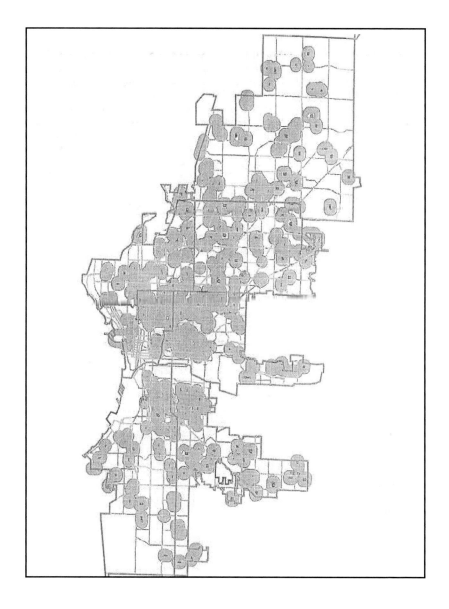

Be A **Victim**

or

Be A **Survivor**

LEOSA Trainers, Inc.